# A Grotesque Animal

# A Grotesque Animal

Amy Lee Lillard

UNIVERSITY OF IOWA PRESS, IOWA CITY

University of Iowa Press, Iowa City 52242

uipress.uiowa.edu
Printed in the United States of America

isbn: 978-1-60938-957-4 (pbk)
isbn: 978-1-60938-958-1 (ebk)
Design and typesetting by Erin Kirk



Printed on acid-free paper

Cataloging-in-Publication data is on file at the Library of Congress.

For all the weird women

# Contents

# Author's Note

Memory is mercurial. Feeling and experience are downright witchy. These essays come from my experience, and feeling, and memory. And while truth is increasingly perceived as relative, I have worked to be as truthful and accurate as possible. Most names have been changed, and some small details have been conflated or altered for readability and protection.

Please note: there is discussion of mental health, depression, and suicide in these pages. There is emotional trauma, complex post-traumatic stress disorder, and tough family dynamics. There is analysis of bodies, sex, and coercion.

# Part 1 Masked Woman

# The Narrator

*I am a narrator*. The line came to me years ago, and I wrote it down in a notebook holding other phrases and ideas and images. I didn't know what it meant, but I knew how it felt. Something locking into place, something inherently right. Anyone who creates anything knows that feeling.

I tried to understand the line by putting it in stories, by writing novels around it. I made it science fiction and magical realism and painful realism, but nothing truly worked. For years, it was one of many lines and phrases and stories that lived on unread pages. And that seemed to be that.

Every story, all of our favorite stories, has a narrator. They can be the main character, who recounts the story with an infallible, photographic memory. They can be multiple people, vying to tell their side. The narrator can be alive or dead; they can be magic or desperately real; they can be trustworthy or they can be telling you lies.

But ultimately, the narrator is created by the author. The narrator is constructed as a voice in which to tell the story. The narrator is often, never, always, a stand-in for the author.

I usually write fiction. There are a million annoying debates among fiction writers about the right kinds of narrators, the right kinds of voices and styles, and blah blah blah. When you're starting out, learning, practicing, trying new stuff, you get dizzy with all the debate. You try it all, for better or worse.

And eventually you find your own way (along with the growing certainty that most of the people arguing don't actually write).

When I write fiction, I create narrators who feel right for that wholly fantastical tale I'm about to tell. Sometimes it works, and sometimes I have to try again. It can be frustrating, and fascinating. But ultimately, it's no big deal, because it's all made up anyway.

But now, I'm doing something weird. I'm writing nonfiction, the supposed truth. I'm writing about my life and certain experiences within it.

And with this new type of writing, I've entered a realm of more annoying debates and saccharine, pithy sayings. All declaring the kind of narrator needed in nonfiction.

If you're confused, so was I. Isn't nonfiction telling the truth? I can dress it up in pretty words, and use some cool formats, and analyze a couple moments to draw out something universal about life. I can tell the truth in all sorts of unique and surprising ways, and in this thing, this book, I do. So why do I need an intermediary? Why do I need a narrator when it's me writing about me?

And why did I ask these questions, which are the wrong ones?

The misunderstanding, the confusion, makes sense in a telling, poignant way. I discovered at the ludicrously late age of forty-three that I'm autistic. Confusion has been a lifelong, daily, constant experience for me.

When I discovered this fact about my brain, I also learned that all the difficulties I've long had with relationships, both platonic and romantic, were not just me being irrevocably odd and broken. I learned that my sensory struggles, with rooms full of too many people and terrible lighting and odd sounds, were not just me being sensitive. I learned that all the other stuff I've struggled with—depression and panic and IBS and eating disorders and on and on, all of it—were tied to having a disability and not knowing it, to crushing myself to fit into a world not made for me.

And I found I'm not alone. There's a population of women like me, who are, later in life, discovering the word for how we're different. We grew up in a time before autism was discussed, before the great vaccine debates that created the clusterfuck of pandemic fighting and resurgence of eradicated diseases.



As a kid, struggling without knowing why, the only word I knew to call myself was "weird." And that meant danger.

We're animals, all of us. We are animals with instincts that struggle to be heard in our bizarre world of money and politics and gender rules and impending climate doom.

But some evolutionary instinct, something designed to keep me from falling behind and being eaten by a lion or wooly mammoth or T. rex, came out when I was a kid. It made me hide.

Difference is danger; herd mentality and action are safety. The animal rules are simple and cruel. We learn them from our ancestors and those around us. And the penalty for living outside the rules is bloody death.

Being a weird girl in the middle of a small city in a conformist state in a dangerous country in an inconceivable world threatened survival. So I hid my weird. I emulated what I saw other girls do, and what my parents wanted, and what got me praise versus rebuke.

Before my middle-aged discovery, I never considered writing personal nonfiction. I always wrote, though; from an early age I was writing teen melodramas and pop songs and sitcom episodes, taking in what I was reading and watching and trying to do what those people did. I loved it. I wanted to do only that—read and write.

My family was very practical, working-class, and midwestern: college was unnecessary and showing off; jobs were hard and miserable and dangerous; life was limited. When I did the unthinkable—went to college, and later moved away from Iowa, looking for some kind of life I could stomach—I still carried those lessons. I limited myself. Writing was not a career. Writing was not a job. Writing was not something realistic.

So I cobbled together a career in something realistic—marketing and advertising. Joy was not a matter of concern. Fulfillment was just a fancy word snobs used to show off. Every once in a while, I'd try writing fiction on nights and weekends; every once in a while, I'd dream.

But even those stolen moments and brief fantasies were focused on fiction. Not true stuff.

Because why would I stop playing hide and seek and expose myself to danger? And maybe even more terrifying: Who cared what my life was like?

I say that I only wrote fiction, and it's true. But at the same time, it's not.

Because in the fiction, I brought some of myself. When I was younger, I wrote about girls who felt deeply disconnected from the world. I wrote about girls who had extremely difficult relationships with their mothers and strained relations with their fathers. I wrote about girls who became women too soon. Later, I wrote about women who found their queerness late, who experienced abuse, who had affairs, who were suicidal, who had drinking problems, who were desperate to be seen. It was all true, but it was also fiction. Because I could change details, and I could give my characters resolve and closure. I could write who I wanted to be.

And I could create narrators who knew everything—the why and how of it all.

It took me forty-three years and a complete accident to discover why I am the way I am. During that time I hid my weirdness as much as possible, from others and from myself. It broke me to do it. Being around other people grew harder and harder. Being in a workplace became untenable. I sickened myself, and drank myself to further sickness as the weight of every day grew heavier. I was breaking down in a society that does not stomach or support breakdowns, that does not let you stop work to tend to yourself, that does not provide any safety net for figuring your shit out, that does not acknowledge weakness and need (which are the same thing). I was breaking down without the luxury of breaking down.

Then I found my name. And since then, I've been trying to stop hiding.

It's a frustrating process, ongoing and never-ending. I'm unlearning decades of self-burial, and that's tied up with so much else, bad shit in the past that made me doubt myself and my story.

I've found so many stories that I want to tell. That I need to tell. That might help others like me. That might help others who aren't like me.

So we come back to the narrator.

Typical narrators know the ending. They also know the secrets, the things we hide and the things that are hidden from us. They are the source of authority and agency.

True authority and agency in my life have been missing. I let myself be truly weird in one key way—choosing not to get married or have kids—because I knew I'd die if I didn't. But in most other things, I mimicked. I studied and copied. I deferred to others. I buried my needs and my biology deep down. Because to be safe, to not be eaten by the mammoth, I had to pretend to be normal.

Now I'm peeling all that away. Now that I know who I am, I'm rethinking authority and agency. I'm rethinking rules for who I should be, and the mandate to be ashamed for not fitting those rules. I'm finding the roots of me and pulling secrets out of the dark.

So I'm working to grant myself authority: to be as weird and different as I need and want to be. I'm working to give myself agency: to see the ugliness and mess and choose to call it beauty.

This is terrifying. The act of renaming and rediscovery, yes, but also this act of writing about this work.

Creating fiction can be a heady thing. The power of knowing, of plotting. True authority and agency. And the knowledge that, no matter what I write, I can claim it all as literature. As untrue. I can hide.

But now—the audacity of writing truth.

I still want to hide. That impulse hasn't gone away. I am still scared of my parents, and I'm still scared of my ex, and I'm still scared of people I know (and people I don't) reading my nonfiction and saying "it wasn't that bad" or "you're lying" or "you're disgusting."

I'm scared of you, the person reading this page, and your disbelief and your judgment and your ability to cue all the other animals to attack.

But I also want to stop hiding. And that impulse, that need, I'm clinging to it.

I am an animal, used to self-camouflage, to freezing under sight of predators, one haunted with the knowledge of the safety of the herd and the inability to keep up.

I am a human, forged by cruelty, tempted by self-annihilation, surviving by hiding under a smile.

I am a woman, a creature made grotesque by the pressures and policing of a world made for men.

And I am a narrator. I've found the home for these words, and they're not in fantasy. They're in me. They're of me, and with me, and now they're here. They're being read.

I am a narrator. To make that true, I'm writing true stories.

I'm the narrator. So let's begin.

# The Masked Woman

### *A Mask*

A mask is a noun. A physical object, inert, yet one that strains to hold symbols and anger and fear and humanity in its stitches. A piece of fabric, worn to protect the face from illness. Unless you're the righteous ones, defying fabric and flaps for a sense of freedom. Like the man at Target, in 2020, standing in line in front of me, jubilation and rage vibrating off his frame. His mask in his hands and not on his face. His eyes, meeting mine. Daring me, any of us, all of us in the line and behind the register partition to say something.

### *To Mask*

A mask is a noun. But it's also a verb. Action. A singular move made, or an ongoing state. It's a nebulous thing, how a physical object, one that already bears the weight of symbol and meaning, now becomes an action, drawing infinitely more judgment.

To mask, for that man in Target during the pandemic, for all the people who protested "I can't breathe" without any hint of irony, for the men who threatened to kidnap a governor over masks, for the people who scaled the walls of the Capitol to support their unmasked despot, is to lie. It's to conceal things, to hide truth. It's inhuman, un-American. It's socialist and fascist and gay, all things not to be borne.

### *? Mask*

There's another element to masking. Both noun and verb. For all the controversy over masks and masking, all those masks can be removed. They are fabric, or polymer, or paint. External to the human body.

What happens when your mask can't be removed? When you don't even know you're wearing a mask?

### *A + A Mask*

A moment, in a long weekend over the Thanksgiving holiday in 2020. On my couch, alone, blissful in that aloneness, chafing at the role of girlfriend to a man who wants me to be around always, wants me to act as stepmom to his kids, to be happy when he calls unexpectedly, be eager to leave my house and see him, be content to sit next to him and lie next to him and fuck him and not watch the clock for the time I can clock out. For reasons I can't explain, reasons I've always known and never been able to justify, I can never relax around partners, around friends, around anyone. The only safe and truly comfortable space is alone. And I know it shouldn't be, and that makes me ashamed.

Alone. On the couch. Reading *Bust Magazine*, as I've done since college in the late 1990s. Always thrilled and piqued by their unique brand of feminism and stories you don't read anywhere else. Like here, this article, a story about a woman who was thirtysomething and discovered she was autistic. And how about that, women can be autistic? Older women can be autistic? How interesting. How odd that the list of aspects she describes, they echo in my head and my chest, reverberate and beat a rhythm that sounds like another heartbeat. How strange that the ways I've always considered myself weird, different, shameful, they're listed here, they're named, a name that starts with the same letter of the name I was given at birth, a name that might have been there, inside, on my tongue, waiting to be spoken, for forty-three years.

All that to say: I read this article about a woman who discovered she's autistic as an adult, and I, in my midlife, recognize myself.

### *A Mask*

A mask is fabric worn to conceal an identity. Batman. Daredevil. The Watchmen. Hooded vigilantes wearing masks to hide their billionaire trust funds, or their super abilities, or their dirty deeds done dirt cheap. The mask is for their protection, as they claim to protect others.

### *To Mask*

To mask, for movie vigilantes, is acceptable. It's necessary, a first step in becoming the person that city or borough or nation needs, someone braver, stronger, harder, crueler. With this necessity, though, comes existential crisis. Batman is always worried about who's the man and who's the mask. Because they are different. Because a mask is a lie.

### *A + A Mask*

That first day, after reading the *Bust* article, I pull out my phone with a numbness that hurts, and I pull up an online diagnostic quiz. I answer questions about social behavior, relationship behavior, sensory sensitivity, the ways I think and feel and act. And with those answers, the internet adds and subtracts and multiples and divides, and my result is "severe autism."

I take another quiz. Another. Another. Another. Each time, wanting the answer to be both things—that I'm wrong, and that I'm right. Each time, getting an answer that says severe, strong likelihood, get help.

I get up. Walk upstairs to the bathroom, walk downstairs to the kitchen and eat something without tasting it. Open Instagram, close Instagram. Play with my cats. Sit at the dining room table and stare into space.

Then I'm on my computer again, and I'm reading everything about autism, and particularly autism in girls and women, and especially late-diagnosed autism in women. Within hours, I know. This is the word for who I am, who I've been, who I never knew I was but also knew intimately, deeply, at my core. The word for who I really am.

And that means the person I think I am, the person I show to the world, the person I have created, is a mask.

### *A Quick Mask Primer*

Here's what I learn in that fugue state of relentless discovery. Autism is:

- a developmental disability, something passed down through the random stone-throwing lottery of genetics.
- a condition affecting how people think, feel, act, communicate, perceive, and even move.
- a spectrum, meaning behaviors will manifest differently among individuals and across cultures and genders.
- an example of deep medical bias; all the diagnostic criteria were developed using boys, meaning (white) boys are the majority of diagnoses.
- a thing many people and parents want to cure, because the behaviors don't fit nicely into a capitalist, production-driven society, and because our society doesn't like difference.
- a condition that is certainly, fully, maddeningly different than what you think it is.

As I read, that day and for many days after, I understand some key things.

I was born in 1977; in the 1980s and 1990s, autism was not something known widely or discussed beyond "that guy in *Rain Man*." And in that time, and since, as autism has become a lightning rod topic tied to vaccines and cures, the general assumption is that autism is a young white boy, not a grown-ass woman.

Which means, grown-ass women with autism can become hiders. Become hidden.

I was taught to be a girl, which means to be pleasing and self-effacing and normal, and then I was taught to be a woman, which means all those things to exponential values, and I was taught that if you feel bad, physically or mentally, you hide it, because no one will believe you anyway, and I was taught that if I was teased, or bullied, or raped, that I deserved it due to suspect behavior, and I needed to work harder to be who the world wants.

The things typically associated with autism—tantrums, outbursts, monotones, actions that are otherwise abrasive and unpleasant and domineering—are the behaviors of a gender who is prized first, who is allowed to act out, who is forgiven with *boys will be boys*. Those behaviors, that kind of autism, they're beat out of us girls at a very early age. So my autism looks completely different, covered with a mask.

### *A Mask*

A mask is a beauty tool, a cosmetic cream or paste slathered on one's face, with the goal of a before/after reveal. Me, swiping black clay across my cheeks and nose, or arranging a thin wet paper to match my eyeholes and mouth hole, or, back in the day, applying Bioré strips across my nose and chin. Peeling each item off, slowly, feeling soft hairs and bits of skin go with it. Searching for that more beautiful face, the one that will make me happy, or pleasing to others, and really, aren't they supposed to be the same?

### *To Mask*

For a lot of women, to mask is a necessity. Beauty is everything. A pleasing face is all things. A woman must mask to remove all the shit from her face, and then she must put a whole bunch more shit on her face to be acknowledged. But at the same time, you have some men who accuse women of being liars, bait-and-switchers, when they find out how much shit is on their face.

### *A + A Mask*

I read and mark this quote:

> Women with autism are a lot more "autistic" than they look . . . the majority of these women are getting through each day with an often sophisticated set of compensatory behaviors, personas and clever strategies for avoiding certain situations without anyone knowing. Their ability to do this is testament to an extraordinary resilience and sometimes stubborn determination not to "fail"

> or be "outed" as a "weirdo." Unfortunately, these efforts can come at a price: exhaustion, breakdown and other mental health issues are commonly mentioned by these women. . . . Life with autism can break a person. (Sarah Hendrickx, *Women and Girls with Autism Spectrum Disorder* [London: Jessica Kingsley, 2015], 125–26)

I have bent myself backward and sideways to hide my oddness, my unpleasantness; I have studied others to see what normal looks like; I have worked very hard, knowingly and unknowingly, to create a new self, one that I can show to the world. All to be able to live in it.

That's the mask, noun and verb, for a lot of autistic women. It's survival.

## *My Mask*

After my deep dive on that first day, I did two things. I scheduled an appointment with a therapist for assessment and confirmation. Then I told two people via text.

The first was a close friend, one I expected would be as shocked and intrigued as me. And I was right; our conversation was warm, and friendly, and encouraging, and empowering.

The other text was to the man I was dating. He was a man who I had an instinct about from the start, one who I understood was seeing who he wanted to see: a sexually free girlfriend who didn't want to get married, a woman who was passably intelligent, a human presence he could tell all the mundane details of his day, a person who could share the load with his kids. He ignored the true things about me: that I didn't want kids or stepkids, that I didn't want to be a girlfriend, that I chafed at the patterns he was setting up for us. He talked at length, every week, about his budgets and diet; I got a book deal two months into dating, and he said how nice it was to have a hobby.

But I stayed with him, because everyone around me said he seemed so nice, so perfect for me. I stayed, even as I grew increasingly anxious around him, popping lorazepam before our dates, psyching myself up for sex, holding my face still or frozen in a smile.

I didn't yet understand he was a prime example of how autism played a role in my relationships. How much I needed others' voices to tell me how to be.

But I did know I was feeling guilty for not spending more time with him over the long holiday, for starting to pull away from him. So I texted him this new discovery, this fascinating idea that I may have found my true identity. I did it as a bit of intimacy. Look, my subtext said. Look, I'm sharing myself with you, as you've asked. I'm being honest and open. I'm trusting you. Look: I've found the real me.

His texts were often long, maddeningly and boringly detailed, filled with the minutiae of his day. The text on this day was just a few words. "That's interesting." Or maybe, "Huh, that's strange." Or maybe, "That's something." The truth is lost to text deletion, a purge after I'd finally cut him loose months later. But the sentiment, and the length, are there. As is the silence, the refusal to talk about it any further, then and after. The skepticism plain and pointed.

It was the first time, and not the last, that I understood how well I had masked. How realistic I'd made my mask. How thoroughly it fit. How much it appealed. It was the first time, and not the last, that I'd see how some people believed my mask and not me. How some people would not, and will not, see *me*.

### *A Mask Primer*

Masks can be nouns and verbs. They can also, as a subgroup of both, be names and labels.

When I conducted my frenzy of initial online testing, the results often gave me a label, like "severe" autism. Later in my research, I would find more labels, like "high functioning." Months later, when I went public with my discovery and diagnosis, I would hear more words people used to describe my identity and the act of sharing it: brave, bold, special, pure, surprising. Or, I heard the most resounding and resolute of silences.

All that language and its lack to say: my mask was a good mask. It was a pleasing mask. One that denied its existence as a mask. One that said this woman, this one right here, this one admitting she's disabled; she doesn't need anything, doesn't demand we change anything. She has contorted herself to fit in with us, the normal and righteous members of this world. And thus, we deem her acceptable. While we will also remember this information, and change our tones, and understand her to be less than, and this will be reflected in our language that indicates she is now a pitiable, infantilized *other*.

I read and marked this passage.

> At some point in their lives, often when adult responsibilities become too much, the amount of energy required to continue pretending, or "passing," simply becomes too much. Depression, burnout, fatigue, and anxiety frequently surface. Women are often unaware that such pretending and mimicking are even happening. But as they need more mental energy in more and more areas of life . . . it becomes clear that there has been a long-standing disconnect between their actual inclinations and the ways in which they have acted out of social obligation. (Jenara Nerenberg, *Divergent Mind* [New York: Harper & Row, 2020], 80–81)

And really, what else can we expect? When it's been clear what the world demands of us women? If we were born two hundred years ago, we'd be called hysterical. If we were born three hundred years ago, we'd be called witches.

So. Labels are a code that say: You, hiding your autism so well, how cute and quirky you are to admit it, when you know we'll pity you for it.

Or.

You, you woman, you daughter, you relative, you friend, telling a story about being disabled to get attention. You. You don't deserve to be acknowledged. This does not deserve discussion or recognition. You. Who do you think you are?

## *A + A Mask*

My new name came with a sort of relief. An understanding that calmed. But it also came with grief. Even rage.

I knew I wore a mask. But I didn't know where its edges were. I didn't know how to take it off. I didn't know what I would find underneath.

Masking for an undiagnosed autistic woman is often survival. It's a daily, minute-by-minute act. And when I learned that I was masking so hard and so well I didn't know how to stop, and that few people believed that truth, survival became an element of doubt.

In the months after my therapist confirmed I was autistic, I isolated. I withdrew. I dragged myself through the bare minimum of actions to retain a salary. I made checklists to guide me through a day, with things like "feed cats," "take shower," "eat." My body felt skinless, raw and exposed. My house became a fortress, with me hidden in its keep.

At the same time, I was promoting my first book, conducting interviews where I slipped on that mask of sanity and levity. I cracked jokes and smiled and agreed that this was so exciting, so wonderful, this thing I'd worked my whole life toward. I was pleasant and thoughtful and reciprocal. And then, when I got home, or when I closed Zoom, I slumped down and shut down, for hours or days or weeks.

### *? Mask*

Time passed. As it does. And the worst of the weight receded.

Know that this isn't one of those success stories, saccharine and self-congratulatory. The depression happened again the next year, and the year after that, and just a couple months ago. I still feel that weight, and know that I will collapse under it again. Just not today.

### *To Mask*

To mask is an act, and actions incur judgment. It's lying, or it's corrupting, or it's faking. It's associated with actions that some women must take to be in the world, and therefore it's suspect.

### *A Mask*

A mask is a noun. It's fabric, or plastic, or clay. It's only acceptable on designated holidays, or in rough-and-tumble sports, or in the never-ending quest to be prettier.

When I think about masks as objects, though, I return often to the idea of masks in pop culture. Male superheroes wear a mask to protect themselves while taking justice into their hands. But women in these worlds, the likes of

Wonder Woman, or Buffy the Vampire Slayer, often wear no mask. They are expected to show themselves fully, to allow us to see our rescuer, to watch their hair blow and their tits jiggle, to be seen and judged as they do their work.

That shows who decides the value of masks.

Which means: masks are not the enemy. Tangible masks, or the act of masking, are not inherently bad. People who believe the masks are not bad.

Yet the impetus remains: to consider my own mask an enemy. To want to assign blame for making me mask. To want to cast that injustice at the feet of my parents, or corporate capitalists, or the patriarchy, or ableism. That may all be true.

But. Consider this. My mask has also enabled me to live in the world. And my mask is a work of art. It is something I worked since birth to create. It is a composite of every experience, every confusing social interaction, every painful and mystifying end to friendships, every chaotic sexual relationship, every hidden obsession and fantasy and idiosyncrasy. It is born of intense, masterful observation and analysis of people around me. It is bred from hurt and from secret joy.

And under it is the creator, the entity who survives. Who lives on. It's me. She exists.

# There Is No You

You
What you looking at?
"Head Down," Nine Inch Nails

You're thinking about killing yourself. Because you hurt, body and mind. You've hurt for years, and years, and years. And you're so tired of hurting.

It's not all the time, these thoughts of dying. Sometimes you feel better, almost manic in the joy wrought from a David Bowie song and vegan Ben & Jerry's and a *Battlestar Galactica* rewatch and fat cats cavorting on Instagram.

But sometimes. Music is just noise. Food is cardboard. Art is copies of copies. Animals are all going to die. All of us animals, rotting and seeping, on this overheating, overwrought planet.

There's a moment of overwhelming sadness, of desperation, of feeling so alone. You're scrolling, and through the haze you register social media discussions around suicide awareness. How cute, how maddening, that normal people have to be reminded that suicide exists. You follow a link, find a hotline and prevention group. You are curious, in a detached way, but also in a deeply necessary, hopeful way. Will they have a solution? Some hard-fought wisdom? Proven help?

And glory on high, here is their advice: talk to someone. A family member, a friend, a spouse.

You, a grown woman, deep in your forties. Appalled. What are you to do with this? Because if you could talk to someone, really truly talk, show them the full breadth and depth of your depression, maybe you wouldn't be thinking about the best methods of turning this body to dust. If you could talk to family, maybe the shame over your estrangement would subside. If you could talk to friends, without adding to their own struggles, maybe you'd feel less odd. If you could allow a partner or spouse into your life without a throbbing fear of their abuse or your oblivion, you'd feel less strange.

Those writers, those marketers, those medical professionals. You know with certainty they've never felt the abyss. The pull of negation. They've never been held back from slicing their wrists for a fear of not being found for weeks. They've never felt the crucifying pain of seeking anonymous help and finding a Hallmark missive, reinforcing how alone you really are. You know they have nothing for you. No one does.

*Know your place, don't ever forget*

There are compounding factors, layers, to this drive, this desire to end. You must acknowledge this.

Because feeling alone is one thing. But you, you're a woman. Alone while female is another entity altogether.

A solitary, single woman is abhorrent. A failure and a shame. You're a spinster. An old maid. A cat lady. You're the specter, the ghost of Christmas future, the losing card in a game. You're the pitiable woman with graying hair and sagging belly, the crone knocking around the neighborhood's haunted house all by herself.

The implication: you were never chosen. You were too picky, too prudish, to earn a man. Your more generous critics will acknowledge your bisexuality. How progressive of them. They'll say you were too picky to earn a man *or* a woman. You should have been more accommodating, more loving, more self-effacing. Because now look at you.



The truth: you *were* chosen. Again and again. And you were accommodating and self-negating and all those things you thought women are to be. You lived with men, and loved men and women.

There's no language for women who choose solitude over suffocation.

*What you want, what you get*

There was one partner whom you lived with for ten years. A decade of your life. You chose him, or he chose you and you went along with it. And inertia, society, plate tectonics, they convinced you to stay, to make a home together. Long past the time you understood he viewed you as a thing to crush and control.

Your bed, next to an achingly cold brick wall. You'd go to that bed early, hoping he wouldn't follow. Hold yourself rigid when he finally did. Feign sleep so there was no chance for a fight. Stay up, eyes closed, as he fell asleep. Watch the shapes behind your eyelids, watch as film played of your happy arm-in-arm public appearances, followed by images of him looming, whispering brutal nothings, issuing rules and punishments, so that he could sculpt the woman he wanted from the slab of you.

Sometimes you wondered if he was your inner shame made manifest. If you imagined him. If you made up the wonderful, progressive guy all your friends knew, or the secret guy who only you knew. Sometimes you wondered if you were real; if you were the shapes behind your lids, or the body that trained itself to stay still while sleeping.

You stayed with him, though. What does that say about you?

*Bet you didn't think it would happen to you*

So yeah, romantic relationships didn't protect you or sustain you, didn't shield you from being alone. In truth, you never felt more alone than when you shared that bed with a living, breathing human next to you.

After the fallout of that decade, after breaking down and building yourself up again, after you stopped having nightmares of being trapped in that bed (for a while, anyway), you're okay without a person.

And remember. Even when you were partnered, you didn't want marriage. Didn't want to lose your name and identity to legality and custom. Didn't want your dad to walk you down the aisle like a prize steer.

That certainty, that felt good. So did the knowledge that you never wanted children. You've already raised children, really. You were in elementary school when your harried, too-young parents deemed you the guardian of your toddler twin brothers. You were in middle school when you were farmed out as cheap childcare to your working-class neighborhood. You spent long adolescent summer days trapped with babies and kids and an unmoving clock.

No. No kids for you. And what a relief that has been.

Except so many wonder what to make of a grown woman without children. Who do you think you are? Not a real woman, that's for sure. Not a useful woman. Not a full member of society.

You try not to, but you internalize that. And you try to find another purpose besides mothering. Like writing. Telling stories, making a mark that will live on. And you do it. You write and work and hustle and push and teach yourself and persist. You get book deals, and you publish books. Fucking books, just like you dreamed about as a kid.

But it means nothing, not really. You're still a sad failure at the things that matter. You're still a selfish shame to family, an odd burden to friends. You spend all this time on books that change nothing, that don't make your family love you or people understand you. So now you're spent and empty. Now you ask yourself that question: Who do you think you are? And the answer is a blank echo, a resounding silence.



*Know your place, don't ever forget*

The only safe place is alone. That's what your past partnerships taught you.

That's also what your family taught you, people who don't understand or condone difference. They think you seek attention, that you court misery by stubbornness and identity politics. Your mother doesn't speak to you. Your father has another family he prefers. Your brothers believe you'd be better, less selfish, less self-absorbed if you had kids like them.

That's also what friendships taught you. You've had them, weak and paltry things that easily snapped. For years, you couldn't keep friends and couldn't understand why. Now in middle age, you finally have solid friendships. A chosen family. They're the misfits and the gays and those who have contended with their own turmoil and survived. They know you're a bit prickly, a bit strange. They accept you. But they're almost all partnered or married. Some are parents. You're still odd. Alone.

That's what years of assault by the physical world, the sensory world, the work world, taught you. That's what the bomb in your brain, the hidden wiring, the sabotage that only earned a name after forty-some years, taught you.

And that's fine. You can live with alone. You can happily be a spinster, an old maid, a cat lady. You can be whatever people think, because they don't really exist.

So you detach from everyone, push away and pull away. No one understands. No one can bear your extra weight. No one is really real. Only you.

But sometimes, you can desperately wish it was different.

*And this is not my face and this is not my life*

The first time you catch yourself thinking about killing your body, to long for it, to feel the deep sigh of relief at just the prospect of it, the alarm bells ring in your head. Warning, abort, danger. Forbidden. You back away slowly.

But the containment has been breached, and each time after your thinking goes further. You ignore the alarms until they cease. It's easier every time.

Because each downtime gets deeper. Darker. In days gone, you'd drink, and scream at blistering punk shows, and smoke, and repeat. Now you take pills, and you work with a therapist. But still color leeches from your world. You've been through this before. You've experienced depression and anxiety and panic since you were a child. But it's only grown older, stronger, meaner.

You've become more and more adept at directing your sadness, your desperation, your pain inward. And you've also become an expert at directing your anger, that most potent of feelings, inward. Everything, your anger, your sadness, your pain, pushed inside, until your skin cracks and peels and your head threatens to fracture. Until your hands twitch, aching to act, to cut, to slice, to relieve the pressure, to end this too-slow breaking.

You get practical, filling mental spreadsheets with tasks to complete before you kill yourself, creating a deck with side-by-side comparisons of methods.

You have to admit—the physical act of murdering yourself scares you. The pain, for sure. But you, you decades-long atheist, you must also admit that you fear the myths of the afterlife. You know humans have warped the same old creation myths again and again to suit their politics and their dominion. But what if there is something?

Set aside religion. What if the true laws of the universe, of physics, of biology, stand firm? The law of conservation of mass, stating that no matter is ever truly created or destroyed, just recycled? Does that mean you'll be reincarnated? What if you get born again, in the dark and terrible future, and life is so much worse?

The fears are there. But so is the hurt. So the idea of an end, a deep final sleep, still appeals. The door is open, the gap wider every time.

*And there is not a single thing here I can recognize*

And then what?

You've unlocked something. You can see a different dimension, accessed only by the few. This reality is overlaid on the real world. Your Gen X brain thinks of VH1 Pop-Up Videos, small bubbles appearing over music videos with trivia and backstory. Only these bubbles point you to other skin that's cracking, other bodies whose souls long to leave. Survivors, of abuse, of trauma, of war and hate and grief. Humans with the language for their pain, and without. People with vision that transcends the normal, the everyday, with stories that brand them and sustain them.

And the bubbles, they point you down a broken, crooked path, to a group of people with brains that work in broken and crooked ways. There's a word they use, a demonized word, a word you never thought would apply to you and your old and female form. But this word you come to understand, to recognize, to accept as your own.

And you find relief in having a word to describe so much of your difference. You find succor in knowing that your brain was not made for this harsh, loud, often cruel world. Of all the words you've found over the years to capture a feeling and way of being—queer, bisexual, child-free, weird—autistic feels the most revolutionary.

*And this is all a dream*
*And none of you are real*

To confirm your suspicions, you work with a therapist. She runs you through worksheets and guided conversations, and agrees. Your behavior, your patterns, your physiological responses, they all point to autism. A biological difference that's been hiding in plain sight for four decades.

But there's one area she calls out that doesn't match the spectrum. Autistic people often have very good memories. Clear recall of events and experiences, transcending normal. But you, you don't. Your memory is filled with black, blank spots lasting years. Fragments that intrigue and terrify. This is a response to trauma, she says.

You push back. You've not fought a war, or been the victim of a massive crime, or any of the things we now acknowledge as hard and inhuman, deserving of an official diagnosis of PTSD. You can't own that term. You don't deserve it. It wasn't that bad.

There's big T trauma, she says. Singular, massive events. And there's little t trauma. Sustained, over time, rinsed and repeated. Your trauma is from living in a world not meant for you, and living in a family who didn't see you, and living in relationships that hurt you. The body feels this complex trauma. Remembers it. Recycles it into anxiety and depression and IBS and eating disorders and all the things wrong with you.

So you begin work, you and your therapist. Talking about the things you remember, and the things you don't. Digging into and dissecting where autism has affected you, where trauma has hurt, and where the two interact in complementary or contradictory ways. It's powerful, and it's terrible. And each time you remember—your brain is actually different. Plus you've lived through some hard stuff. The therapist is right. It's a comfort.

This fact is also an added pain. Because autism is permanent. This is body and brain. You've named your differences, but there's no fixing them. You weren't made for this world. That's devastating. And lonely.

And in moments when you are bombarded by memories returning, dug up from the careful and compassionate work of therapy, and you name bad shit as bad, and you understand how hard it still is, and may continue to be, you are raw. You work to remove your mask and tear the skin off with it. You walk around as a seeping open sore, expected to smile with a skinless mouth.

And you see no future of peace. You remember the world is heating up and tearing apart, and your country is transforming under the guidance of mercenary fundamentalists, and you still live paycheck to paycheck, and there will be no safety as you grow older and unable to work.

You're an animal, in a crouch. Alert, watchful, wary. Ready to flee, even if that's into the dark dark. Which seems like a viable plan, the only plan. Maybe not now. But someday. It will happen; it has to happen.

And that certainty, how do you live with it?

*You, what you looking at?*

Something will shift.

It always does. The world will come back into view, pull you up from your abyss. Maybe it's the cat that jumps on your lap, her purr a balm. Maybe it's a song you'd forgotten, played at top volume to raise the hairs on your arms and bring out your tears. Maybe it's a filthy funny meme sent in a group text.

And you'll survive this round. You'll delay the inevitable. For now, today.

And maybe that will be enough to spur you to action. To get another tattoo, remaking your body into a work of art, something you don't want to turn into ash. To allow a friend to make you laugh so hard your head aches. To recognize and realize that this, this pain you endure yet again, is not you alone. There are others who feel it too.

And maybe, you can transform pain into art, like so many who wrote the books you grew up on, that inspire and thrill you. Art that might help others feel less alone.

Like this. This thing you've written. This piece that you've framed as a message to yourself. This fragment that's also speaking directly to those who read it. To make sense of it all. To comfort. To hug. To remind.

The thrumming beat of Nine Inch Nails behind you, you hurt. You do. And you feel alone, because it's just you and the music and your words. You think there is no you reading this. There is only me.

But now, in this moment, you want it to be different. You will it to be different. You will the existence of a reader you. You will yourself to be more than just me. You will it all to be worth it. You hope. That's something.

# Part 2 Trashy Woman

# Flex and Point

~~In *Back to the Future*, one of many movies I watch over and over on VHS as a kid, Marty McFly examines a picture of himself and his siblings after time-travel mishaps. His brother's head is gone. "Erased . . . from existence," says Doc Brown.~~

When I'm little, and my mom comes home from work, she strips off her early 1980s working woman uniform. The cheap skirt suit, the pantyhose, and the heels. Her body is marked by tight seams and feet warped by triangle toes. All day she has held herself tight, a smiling, helpful worker. No complaints.

Now she breathes. She scratches her belly and her C-section scar. She's so young; at twenty-six, she's a mother of a six-year-old and toddler twins. She's scrounging, trying to pay for it all with her bank teller wages and my dad's new police gig. She's trapped in a cage she chose. She looks in the mirror, as I hide in the doorframe. She sighs.

The moment is brief. Because then she's up again, to put on a loose shirt and jeans. Off to her second job as the family maid, cook, and laundress.

During this shift, my mother lets loose. Anger pours out of her, into the tater tot casserole and beef and noodles. It runs across her skin like static in Midwest winters. It comes out as screams, or tears, easily, quickly, at the dinner table, at the TV, at bedtime. Directed at us, at me.

It's ugly and scary and embarrassing and confusing.

Then, after the second shift, and the explosion of emotion, there's still more work to be done. Everyone goes to bed, and she goes to the basement, next to my bedroom, and puts her Jane Fonda workout tape into the VCR. As I lay in bed, listening to Jane exhort all the working women to flex and point, my mom punishes her body in the dark. Remembering the tightness of her hosiery, the lack of give in her skirts. The fear of legs rubbing together, of belly sagging, of numbers on a scale.

Because a woman can do all the work, but must still take up the least amount of space.

Each night, I have a grotesque vision of the future. This explosion my mom can't control, this never-ending work, this effort that's rendered invisible, this tight hold that cannot hold: that's what it means to be a woman.

~~Erasing is analog. Today nothing is really erased. We can delete files and photos and everything digital, but we can always retrieve them.~~

My young, tired, angry mom, she works outside the home, like all the women in my family, like more and more women in the early 1980s. She is defined by her work; she works hard for the money, and she's workin' nine to five, and she has to work work work work work, and she don't wanna do your dirty work, and yet she's still gotta work, bitch.

But at her job, and in her home, she also does the work men don't want to do. The work of life that men just expect to get done. The work of living with men: cleaning up their messes, listening to their tantrums, mothering them. The work that is unpaid, unacknowledged.

Getting angry at men is pointless. She's a bitch if she does. A problem. She's punished by cheating, belittling, stagnating. The exhaustion behind the anger and sadness, the eraser rubbing her out.

So instead of directing her anger at men, she fights with other women. Especially her family.

~~But get yourself a rubber eraser and you can wreak havoc.~~

When I'm little, and when I'm less little, and when I'm grown, the women in my maternal line are all angry. Always half a second away from eruption. My mother's anger is a thing to fear, and her sister's anger is a thing to fear, and their mother's anger is a thing to fear. Anger, the hot lick of it, the spontaneous, unpredictable spark of it, passes from one to the other.

They turn their anger on those below them. There is no point in punching up; while they feel powerless, over men, over their body, over their jobs, over their despair, there's no way to change that. But there's always someone below them. They're white, so they can attack brown and Black. They're native, so they attack immigrants. The queers, the fatties, the cripples, the ones who speak different and eat different and worship different. And perhaps worst of all—the people who ask for help. Welfare? Affirmative action? Gender equality amendments? Please. They had no help. Why should others? Anyone asking was lazy, pathetic, weak.

They turn their anger on other women, using a particular vocabulary: fat bitch, uppity bitch, rich bitch, n-word bitch.

They turn their anger on each other, and on me. And they turn it into an identity. They joke about their hot tempers, their trashiness, their toughness. They joke about not having a choice, since we're all redheads—red is wild, it's blood, it's violent. Brazen and bright. Dangerous and sinful. They present to me their rage, their fighting, their working-class fire, present it as a genetic mantle I will take up, the next redhead in line. They give it to me as a birthright, an impotent and futile gift that will eat us all alive.

Their anger transforms. It turns into outbursts, acting out. It turns into one-upping and oversharing. It turns into dick jokes in front of evangelical in-laws, spiteful rides on motorcycles with bad guys, alcoholism and drug abuse, sexual hijinks. Combined with their constant work, their neighborhoods, and their lack of money, their anger and its mutations turn into a reputation we'll never escape: utter trash.

~~Apply some pressure and you can obliterate whatever you want.~~

My mom, aunt, and grandma, as much as they're brash and mad and wild, they're also deeply susceptible to what the world tells them. No matter the anger and the acting out, they ultimately do what they're supposed to: marry husbands who watch TV while the women clean; work at their low-paid jobs at auto dealers and typing pools and banks; put their face on every morning.

And they erase themselves as they go. The women in my family, they say, and believe, the things they've heard:

It's not that bad.
It was just a joke.
I can do it all.
It didn't hurt.
I can't help that woman.
I'm alone in this.
I'm not that kind of woman.
I'm not like her.
I'm not a feminazi, but.
I had it hard; why shouldn't she?
I'm nothing without a family.
I'm not hungry.
I'm not angry.
I'm fine.
I'm fine.
I'm fine.

~~The words you write, the image you draw, transformed to thin shards of rubber and paper.~~

This was the narrative I told myself for years—my angry, bitter, slutty, trashy family of women who were desperately angry and secretly sad, and the lessons I learned about how to be a woman. This was the reason for our difficult, strained connections that often turned into complete pissed-off silence.

I used this narrative to explain, in part, why I chose to live a life without children or a spouse. I thought this would free me from the rage and sadness of my mother, my aunt, my grandmother. From the self-sacrifice and erasure.

But I worked too, early and often. As a kid, I babysat my brothers and the kids in the neighborhood. As a teen I worked as a grocery store grunt. As a college student, the first in my family, I worked everywhere—pizza places, computer labs, telemarketing firms, dog sitting, research, on and on.

Then I moved away and began a new life in Chicago. Thinking I'd escaped fate. Thinking all that work prepared me for something better: a better career, an easier life. I'd be different.

My first corporate job had tons of perks but little salary, tons of responsibility and mandated hours but little autonomy. My next jobs had variations on that theme. At those jobs I developed a fear of meetings and group tasks. I avoided events, calls, lunches, and new, unplanned activities. I heard that I was too blunt. I felt the fluorescent lighting seep into my skin, the beige walls reflect back on my eyes in dizzying ways, the open office plans and hints of cubicles tear away at my crust, flay me until I sat skinless and raw.

And I had a partner, and I became his caretaker and therapist, working additional shifts, disappearing within myself.

And I had my creative dream, so I worked on the side, scrounging, writing for exposure, falling for scams, until I gave up.

I developed a drinking problem, the kind where I clung to the idea that I didn't drink every day, and on the days I did drink, I started after noon, and thus was not an alcoholic.

Over twenty years, pressure built. I didn't melt down, not at first, because for ten of those years I was in a relationship that would not have allowed it, built around his moods and not mine. But when I left him, when I finally ran, the bill came due.

I took multiple trips to the office bathroom every day to cry and rage. I drank more. I pushed myself on longer and longer runs, ate less and less. I fucked a lot of men and women. I finally left the city, found somewhere to hide.

And increasingly, I felt a bubbling, volcanic anger. A genetic, gendered ache from the violent swipes of the eraser, yes. But also a deep rage that I couldn't explain, that would overtake me, inhabit me.

All that time, though, I functioned. I produced. I did what I had to do to keep a salary, to keep going. Because I'm a woman, told over and over again to work, work, work, work, work, no matter the pain or inner turmoil, to deny yourself, erase yourself, sacrifice yourself. Because there are no breaks when you're a woman, and there are no safety nets when you're in the United States, and there is no money in our family, anywhere, from any generation, to ease the crush. Because admitting difficulty is weakness, and disability is exit from normal society. Because the world is designed to crush, to break, to exalt a few over many.

And me, I was nobody. Just like them, the women before me. Our lives served to sell us on that truth. Our mandate to shut up and carry on.

~~The act of erasing is inherently violent. If you rub too hard you can burn your way through the surface, create a hole in the loose-leaf paper.~~

Because I did that, and because I know how it felt to live without knowing why things were so difficult for me, and because now I know who I've always been, I look back with new eyes at the truths of the women in my family.

There's a problem here: I can't talk to any of them about this. My grandmother is dead. My aunt is who knows where. My mother and I don't speak. So I can't ask them about their lived experiences, the ways they felt (and feel) when they lashed out in anger or melted down in tears and rage. I can't ask about the ways their senses registered the world, how they knew their work was never done. I can't share what I've learned about autism and the ways it makes me who I am. I can't offer this word to them to see if it fits.

We share the recessive gene of red hair; do we also share the gene for autism? Do we also share the experience of living in a world designed to break us, in a world that didn't know or accept that autism existed, let alone autistic women?

I put them in my place, with a brain that processes sensory input a bit differently, which causes confusing pain. A brain that processes emotions differently, meaning they rise and fall quickly, unbidden, unclear. A brain baffled by social relationships, with a history of broken friendships and a tendency to use oversharing and brashness as cover for awkwardness and pain.

I put them in my place, with all these truths mixed, combined, catalyzed. And the understanding that I must hide.

And I put myself in their place, when the pressure cannot stand but releases in unexpected ways. Lashing out. Melting down. At others, family, or myself.

And I see their anger anew.

~~Erased . . . from existence.~~

I was angry, and hurting, and deeply, profoundly burned out from constant work when I finally read that *Bust* article and found my name. I found how I'd been erased.

And now I look at the women in my family, at our trashy reputation, our brash and angry personas, and see annihilation. How they worked and worked and worked to be in the world, to be wives, to be moms, to be women, and never knew why it was so fucking hard.

I hold grudges. There's too much damage done. But I also feel protective. I am the only one to find my name. I'm the one who can see past the wild shock-and-awe exterior, to the ghostly imprint on that loose-leaf paper, to what lies underneath.

And in the process, I can make sure we're not erased.

# Maps of the World

When I'm eight years old, I walk the mile home from elementary school alone. I use my key and I take care of myself while my dad, who works night shifts as a police officer, sleeps in his bedroom. Basically I'm home alone.

The phone hanging on the wall rings. I pick it up, and there's a man on the other end. He's breathing loud, wet, with a sort of chuckle.

*Are you alone?* he asks.

I'm sure I say yes, trained to always be polite and responsive.

*Do you want to be?*

I'd like to think that I hang up then, despite my conditioning. But maybe I don't. Maybe I hear him laugh again, glory in my fear of being rude. Maybe he says more, shout-whispers the things he wants to do to me.

I think I slip away in that moment, into the black that dominates most memories of my childhood.

At some point, though, I do hang up, because this isn't the end to this story. I might be crying; I might have already learned that crying is weakness. I run down the short hall of our split-level house to stand outside the door to my parents' bedroom. Inside that room, Dad sleeps on my parents' waterbed. I plan to open that door, tell him what happened, be comforted.

When I try to picture that plan, visualize it, find what I'm looking for, I can't see it.

So I stop myself at the end of the hall. Sink down to the carpet and hug my knees.

I never tell anyone.

This story, small and insignificant as it is on the scale of things awful men do to small girls, is a puzzle. And at the end, if I can assess the puzzle correctly, absent a box picture, something important awaits. An answer to the question: What am I afraid of?

It's not feeling alone in my home at age eight. Because it's circa 1985. My dad works. My mom works. Everyone works in the family, in the neighborhood, in the city. Everyone clocking in and out in order to survive. Everyone so young, without college educations, without apparent joy. Just work. Even me—I work. Taking care of myself. Taking care of my toddler twin brothers. Taking care of my parents when they rage, cry, fight, and have no one to talk to but me.

And me, I'm a good girl, quiet, self-sufficient, self-effacing. A little adult. I'll be fine on my own, my parents decide when they consider babysitting costs.

So taking care of myself is normal. And in fact, this alone time, this brief quiet, outside the cacophony of third grade and the chaos of young parents with young kids, is wonderful. I'll have dreams for the rest of my life of that walk to and from school on my own, and the biting worry of losing my key, and the various confusing interactions of the day, and the pressure of being the kid no one worried about. But the time spent on my own: a joy only matched when I get my first apartment by myself in Chicago, and feel true calm.

What am I afraid of?

Picture a string board, like in the shows with tenacious alcoholic detectives and schizophrenic geniuses. And a series of questions, a path that will lead us through the labyrinth, where at the center awaits something true.

Am I afraid of the man on the other end of the phone?

As I said, this is 1985, and I'm a kid in America. So I know all about stranger danger and men in vans with candy and razor blades in that candy. I know about Satanists around every corner. I also know about my city in Iowa, where newspaper boys have disappeared without a trace, and where day-care workers have built chicken coops to cage kids. I know about my country, ready to fire nukes at the Soviets before they fire them at us, burning us all in nuclear fire.

I know adults are dangerous. Here's one on the other end of the phone, his breath and his shaky voice in my ear.

This is something some men did then. This is something some men do now. They scare women and girls, feel their fear in their hearts and dicks. It is a route to power, an easy one for the men who otherwise feel powerless. And it works.

So sure, I'm afraid of him. Because he's not just on the phone; he's out there, maybe at the door, maybe behind the garage. He's been watching me. He's chosen me for his plans. He's probably a neighbor, someone who knows my schedule, knows I'm the only one conscious in the house.

That's objectively scary. Even for a supposedly self-sufficient little girl.

But I don't wake my dad for help or comfort to ease that fear.

So what am I afraid of?

Am I afraid of my dad?

Simple: yes. Because he's a dad, and dads are often scary, and allowed to be scary.

But my dad is more. Our city has vested him with power and authority. Every day I see him put on his bulletproof vest under his black shirt, his gun belt over his black pants. Shiny black shoes and hat. I've touched the gun he points at bad people, the heavy lead asp he uses on bad heads, the nightstick he thrusts into bad guts.

I'll grow up to learn that many police families have stories of terror at home, when the father brings state violence home to his wife, his kids. Dad does not touch us in this way. But he does beat the family dog and once threw a tiny kitten against a wall, has squeezed wasps with pliers. He tells us stories of beating criminals until they are unconscious and bloody, stories designed to make us laugh. He is celebrated for chasing, fighting, beating, screaming, lying, and tricking. He kills a man at work, and his face is everywhere on the news, vilified and celebrated. Later, he'll work undercover in narcotics, bringing home confiscated sports cars, along with pictures of himself with piles of drugs and money and guns. Later still he'll work with SWAT teams, appearing in televised raids. Each new role increasing the fear for and of him.

So maybe I'm afraid of Dad's violence. Unsure where it might be directed when there is not a visible culprit. Protecting myself, sure, but also the animals in the house and the people he might see on the street that night.

Because even at my young age, I know the lines he draws around good and bad guys is blurry. He talks about Black men as the animals of the street. He and Mom and our entire extended family tell jokes about Black people as ignorant, lazy, fat; all the greatest hits of white American racism. He and his police buddies tell the jokes and make the profiles.

Already, I have a different childhood than my parents. Dad grew up in white suburbs and arrested the first Black man he ever met. In this diverse city, on this run-down east side of town my parents can afford, I go to school with Black kids, Vietnamese and Cambodian and Thai kids, Mexican and Salvodoran kids.

So I'm already aware that while Dad has power—more than me, more than most—that power might be suspect. And in that way, he's scary.

Am I actually afraid of disbelief?

If I wake Dad in this moment, tell him about the loud breath and creepy voice on the phone, he will quickly understand. He's part of that world of men, of male voices who enjoy inciting fear in females. The world of men who will explain away other men and the games they play.

Girls make up things, after all. That's what Dad says. Girls lie about the things boys do to them. But also: girls have to protect themselves, because boys will do things to them.

It's dizzying and confusing.

I'm a girl, and girls are not to be trusted. We're sniveling and shaking creatures. We're not tough and hard, like him.

If I was tough and hard, he might respect me and believe me. Tough like Sue, the woman cop he didn't want to work with because women shouldn't be cops. But he was forced, because of goddamn quotas. He hates it, hates how men are being feminized by association. But then, that first night he worked with her, she was brutal. Beating up all the drunks with her nightstick before throwing them in the paddy wagon. A tough butch bitch who outdid them all in violence. That he could get behind.

But I'm not tough, not like that.

So I know I'll get questions if I wake him. What did you do wrong, Amy? Did you answer the phone? Why would you do that? Why are you upset? Why did you let the voice get to you? Why did you wake me for something so small?

You made it all the way home, the mile walk from school, every morning and every afternoon, and no one touched you or kidnapped you or cut your head off. And your dad doesn't touch you in the dark or hit you or keep you locked up.

So what are you crying about?

Am I afraid of something beyond this man on the phone, and the man in my house? Something surrounding the house?

We're in a neighborhood that people in our city consider tough, rough, trash. We get extended coverage on the television news. We get curled lips from my dad's family out in the suburbs. We get heavy breathers to small girls.

Our neighbors are truckers and dairy factory workers and babysitters and firefighters and police officers and moms. Our neighbors sometimes exude danger. Like the drug dealers down the street, where Corvettes and Z28s pull into the driveway at all hours, and where fire trucks appear multiple times to quell their arson attempts. Or like the cult family who wears long denim skirts and hair that goes down to their butts, who homeschool before it becomes a thing, the kids always looking pale and wan, like Confederate widows and Brontë heroines.

There are drunk drivers in our neighborhood too, one of whom plows through our yard and almost crashes into my bedroom. And there are the other criminals, who I'll only learn about as I get older, like the guy from one street north who killed three people, including his daughter.

My dad's father, a brute who beats his wife and cuts down his kids, won't come to our side of town at night. Or really any time. He's a born-again Christian, and he views our side of town as bad, and our mother as bad, and her mother as bad; therefore, us kids are bad too, lost causes who he'll ignore and ridicule in favor of his other grandkids. My dad's mother is meek and small, scandalized by my mom's family, and later me. She follows her husband's lead. As do my dad's siblings, and their kids.

We're the trashy ones in the family, by genetics and by district. And that reminds us, always, of where we fit in the city, in the state, in our lives. A scary proposition.

So am I also afraid, in this moment of huddling in our hallway, of my prescribed future?

Consider this. There's another moment, a couple years out from this phone call. I'm ten years old. I'm with a neighbor who goes to my school. Her dad is a long-haul trucker with a ZZ Top beard and a straw cowboy hat. He calls himself "Wild Bill." Her mom parks us in a vacant lot at night, waiting for him to stow his rig, until someone calls the cops on us.

I'm with the family one day, and we're supposed to go to a pool or something child-appropriate. But on the way we stop at a nondescript building, and inside that building is an anonymous man in a coffin. I don't know this man, don't know why I've been brought to this event called a wake. I do know the man is suited, made up, pretending to be a wax figure, like a powered-down animatronic figure from ShowBiz Pizza. I hear people around us talk about that thing in the coffin, giving him names like *father* and *husband* as they munch cold cuts and potato salad. I watch their mouths move, compare them to his dead tongue.

I've never seen a dead body. I've never seen the people around me. I wonder if this, my friend's parents bringing me to a stranger's wake as if we're getting jerky at a convenience store, is another instance of the reasons people judge us. Why us east siders are all trash. Why we have a very different life from the huge sprawling houses on the west side with their own hard language—gable, gazebo, garden.

The dead man probably lived on the east side his whole life, went to school here, raised kids here, worked at the soybean factory that emitted shit smells into the summer air. He probably smoked cigarettes in an Iowa Hawkeyes T-shirt over a charcoal grill filled with hamburger patties topped with Kraft singles. He probably lived at a house with a tireless car set on blocks in the front yard. He probably felt himself better, a higher class of working class, than the Black east siders, the Mexican day laborers, the Vietnamese, Laotian, and Cambodian refugees. He probably went to sleep with the same east side symphony as us: sirens, revving muscle car motors, bottle rockets, blown-out car speakers shaking the houses they pass, the names of dogs screamed by their owners, the names of children screamed by their parents. He probably said this was life, working and sleeping and smoking and eating.

Someone, somewhere has determined that class is absent from those with less money. Someone has decreed that proper behavior is something different than what goes on over here on the east side. Someone, somehow, has determined that we're the ones who will clean up after others, that we're bound to the gutter.

That man on the phone, he's just showing me, like the dead body will: I'll live and die here, anonymous and angry. I will live in this city, work a job I hate, have family I tolerate, hate anyone else. And even worse: I'll be a girl, lower even than him.

Or. Is this moment of that heavy-breather call something else entirely?

Am I afraid of being caught?

This is around the time that, while I excel at school, I get detention. I'm the first third-grader ever to get detention, an honor usually reserved for fourth- and fifth-graders. And I have no idea why. I hear that I've been mean to someone, that my behavior was out of bounds. And I'm mortified and terrified; the rest of the school year I live in deep, stomach-churning fear that my teachers will tell my mom, or there will be a note on my final report card. That never happens, and I never tell anyone until decades later.

I don't understand what I've done, but this is not new. Most aspects of being around people completely confuse me. I don't understand friendships, how to make them, how to keep them. I don't understand communication, since so much of it is unspoken. I don't understand why others don't notice sounds, smells, sights that I do.

I don't understand many things at this age, but I do understand that I am somehow different. Odd. And difference is dangerous, in the ecosystem of kids and among adults.

Detention is the first prominent, indisputable evidence of this. I've done something terrible, and don't know what it is. So I sit with older kids after school for some sort of punishment (lost to time and black clouds), and let shame collect on my shoulders and sink deep inside the skin.

When this man calls me on the phone and speaks to me in a way that feels off, and I run away scared but keep that fear to myself, maybe I feel like he's found me out. He's spotted me, the weirdo, the bad girl. And he knows that I deserve punishment.

If this is the case, he's the first in a line of men who will determine I'm deserving of less. Who sees I can be manipulated and coerced and hurt. Who I allow to tear me apart.

Or. Maybe this moment is about understanding all of this, together. That I'm afraid of the man on the phone. I'm afraid of being disappointed by my parents, again. I'm afraid of my dad (and my mom). I'm afraid I won't be believed. I'm afraid of being the wrong kind of girl. I'm afraid of being bad, different, wrong. I'm afraid of being weak, easy prey. I'm afraid others will judge me, shame me, for my body, my behavior, my zip code, my latchkey. I'm afraid this is all it, forever and ever amen.

I'm at home, the place I think I feel safe. Until this call, when I understand this is a lie.

Years later, I'll read about women like me, who didn't know they were autistic until adulthood. Many of them found school scary, like me. But for many of them, home was a refuge. Home was a place where, after the confusion and fear of the day, they could let loose. That might mean melting down, or shutting down, or simply letting the stress of the day slip away in favor of comfort and support. Home felt safe.

My home did not feel safe. The people inside, the people outside, the people in the greater world; there was so much to be afraid of. Entire maps of it.

Imprinted on my body and in my body, a latticework of string no one else could see.

And because of that, my mask was always on. I always hid. I disappeared deep within me. Which made it the work of years to dig myself out and find safety.

That day, I cower in the hallway after a man makes me feel small and weak, like the prey I'm destined to be.

After a little while, I get up from outside my parents' bedroom. I probably go do my homework, like a good girl. Soon, Mom will come home, raw and angry from a day wearing heels and the derision of men; soon, Dad will wake, eat the meal Mom prepares, dress, and go to work.

I'll go to bed and start another day.

# The Name of a Universe

*I*

*Singularity*

We don't talk. My mother and I have gone years without speaking. My father and my brothers, we go months until a cursory text check-in or a mandatory Christmas gathering.

When we do speak, the talk isn't real. The things my family and I say to each other are code, run through the encryption of shock and awe, passive aggression, truth or dare.

I have things I want to say. I have questions I want to ask. I want to talk to them, really talk. But there's no precedent. There's no getting past the code; when we venture into real communication, the result is estrangement and silence.

Is this a way to talk to them? This page, and all the pages here? Maybe. But they, my family members, they don't read books. They don't read my books. The likelihood of these pages being discovered, let alone consumed, is slight.

And maybe for that reason, I can be honest. I can get past the code.

*Multiplicity*

When we make decisions, there's the thing we choose, and the thing we don't. We may end up happy with the thing we choose. We may end up furious with ourselves for choosing that thing.

So we pivot back, again and again, to that moment of choice. What would have happened if we chose the other thing? And soon that other thing haunts us. It becomes perfection, beauty, meaning. It promises all the answers. If only.

Sometimes, that other thing can become so real in our heads, we catch glimpses of it. From the corners of our eyes, we see it, see that other life that we could have lived. We start to believe in fantasy, in spirits, because doesn't that other world seem real?

People who steep themselves in science might say that other world we see is real. They might say as vast as our universe is, a vastness beyond our comprehension, it's just one of infinite universes. And each one, each unique universe, is created by a choice.

*Singularity*

My name means beloved. A nice idea for a newborn. This one, the name says. This particular girl. One emerging from another girl in great violence, ripped from that twenty-year-old's belly in an emergency C-section; a baby breathing first breaths in the hot summer in 1977, in a large hospital in a small city in a small state in America. This one, the name says, bears the mark of love.

But names are tricksters. Words, especially when used as markers, are slippery, shifty ideas that resist being held in one place. *Beloved* doesn't specify what love. The word doesn't drill down into how that love is doled out. It takes too much for granted.

I'm born to kids barely out of high school, just as they were to their parents, and they were to their parents. These kids, all of them, they learned there were rules to be loved. Dad learned he must be a sort of midcentury masculine, must prove himself on sports fields, must let his mother get hit, must himself dominate women to be loved. Mom learned she must put on a face, must keep her body thin, must be what a man wants, must get married and have kids to deserve love.

They probably told themselves they'd be different than their parents. They would love their kids wholly. They'd love each other, and that love would grow, and love would be the word when you thought of our family. It was a nice idea.

I didn't understand for a long, long time that love does not have to be transactional, a reward for following rules, a rent charged for lodging in a belly for nine months.

*Multiplicity*

I believe in the multiverse. I type this, and then I read it, and I delete it and retype, because it sounds ignorant. What does belief have to do with science? But in this world people believe in convenience and money. Science gets in the way of that.

In this world, to prioritize something over capitalism feels like a radical statement. It must be said explicitly. In that way, we orient ourselves, understand ourselves to be functioning in the known reality.

I believe in the multiverse, even as I don't fully understand it. It's a matter of numbers, and numbers can get unwieldly, unrealistic.

I can list the big choices of my life—the ones that dictated how I got to this moment in time, this physical place in a house, in a small midwestern city, in a small, strangely politically important state. And when I list them, and list the other choices I could have made, I come up with a web of other worlds.

Where the drawing breaks down, due to my lack of talent and the limits of brain computing power, is within the smaller choices. Is there a world where I ate takeout sushi for dinner last night instead of a PBJ? How different is it? Is there a world where I responded to a work email with profanity and rage instead of the short note couched in corporate speak? And if worlds exist made of all the small, seemingly inconsequential choices of daily life, does that mean those tiny decisions are more important than we realize?

*Singularity*

My name was unique, but it also wasn't. It was the second most popular baby name through most of the 1970s. Which means for most of my childhood and adolescence and early adulthood, I was surrounded by Amys. So I became Amy L. I became my last name. I became Red. All terms to situate me among a sea of similar girls.

My name was chosen to ensure I felt a part of something. Part of a family and part of a community. It was a reminder I was just one of many. My name was expected to do most of the work of making me feel human, because no one in my family knew how to parent. How could they? They were all babies themselves. They were still smarting from the lack of parenting they had, up and up through our genetic line. They were still reeling from the resentment toward their own parents.

My parents' bodies created me, and that should count for something. Their abusive parents and dead parents, their tender teenage youth, their Baby Boomer norms, their sense of entitlement and massive disappointment, their lack of wealth, the names they were called, they created me.

The mothers, my mother and her mother and up and up, they all passed on fear and ignorance and resentment and pain and anger in the amniotic sack. A deep genetic baseline of blood-red rage and the recessive redhead gene. And then, once their children were out in the world, they showed what it meant to live in the world through poorly guided actions.

*Multiplicity*

Science is cold and rigid. Maybe that's why so many people prefer to believe in a kindly white guy up in the heavens, who lashes out when you deserve it.

In science, there is no shame. And maybe that's why so many people prefer to believe in a deity who judges you, deeming you worthy or not. Shame is a great way to keep people in line.

*Singularity*

No one knew how to parent in my family. But even more basic than that: no one knew how to talk. No one knew how to communicate. No one had any clue how to connect.

The talk in my family is hard. As grown-ups, we talk about the drugs we've taken and the sex we've had. The talk is mean. We laugh at each other, call each other names, poke at our soft spots. The talk is oversharing while keeping our vulnerable insides safe. The appearance of closeness, without true honesty.

The talk in my family is also myth-making. My brothers and I, we tell ourselves stories about who we are: east side trash, hard-living and hard-working. We tell stories about the times Dad called us pussies and Mom screamed at us from sports sidelines. We tell stories about who cheated on who in our parents' marriage, and who caused the divorce. We tell stories about each other, gossip framed as concern about my sisters-in-law and their MLMs and social media posturing, my brothers and their manual labor jobs, everyone's drinking.

The talk in my family is also a perpetual game of the Trauma Olympics. Who has it worse? Was it Grandma Kat, with her dead husband and daughters who hated her? Is it Aunt Deb, who seeks love and finds oblivion in one husband after another? Is it Mom, with me as her ungrateful bitch daughter who thinks she's better than her? Is it Dad or my brothers? Is it the stepparents and stepsiblings I don't even include in the conversation?

The talk in my family is sometimes outright lies. It's a tool to win the eternal competitions: Mom versus Dad; Mom versus her sister; Mom versus me. The talk is used to curry favor, elicit sympathy, bring the listener to the speaker's side. It's armor, and it's ammunition. It's propaganda, and state-run newspapers, and Murdoch-owned television news.

The talk in my family is blame. It's guilt. It's demanding a tithe. It's using one another, since we have no one else. Since therapy is pathetic.

The talk is laced with resentment over one central thought: the lives everyone could have lived, if only they hadn't had kids so young.

*Multiplicity*

If parallel worlds exist, if a multiverse exists, in another world a choice was made that changed all this. Somewhere along the line, someone chose to learn about connection. Real communication. Maybe that choice came as a side effect of learning about themselves. Working through the difficult things in their lives and those who came before them. Thinking about their motivations, their struggles, their true selves.

In that world, we know ourselves. We know each other. We are a family who can rely on one another, who can relax into each other, who can restore and provide relief.

*Singularity*

In this world, we have no idea who we really are.

In this world, I'm on edge in every interaction. I'm wary of my words.

In this world, I hurt, and I ache, wishing things were different.

In this world, we betray one another and call it talking.

In this world, we assume a mask with one another, and it becomes permanent armor.

In this world, I use the myth-making, the hard and cold words, the competition, the lies, and I try to make sense of it all. Why we can't connect. Is it all biology? Is it our animal nature? Is it class, and grief, and the doom of the future?

Or is it simply the losing ticket in the multiverse lottery?

## *II*

We always found Grandma Kat at her kitchen table reading mystery novels, doing puzzles, drinking cans of Budweiser at all hours of the day, smoking cigarettes with such stillness the ash would overtake the tobacco.

Kat said things like "fuck him and the horse he rode in on," and "she looks rode hard and put away wet." She said she "had to put her face on," as she penciled eyebrows on her forehead every morning.

She wore her hair cut masculine-short, wore cutoff jean shorts and denim shirts loose around the armpit, offering glimpses of middle-aged breasts.

She walked everywhere in bare calloused feet, roaming her yard like a general, looking for weeds to pull, branches to trim, sticks to collect, seeds to tend.

She drove a black truck with an American flag decal.

She had a black lab, and when that black lab died, she got another black lab the next day, and when that puppy grew up and died, she got another. On and on. They were all named Bucky or Barney or something easily similar.

Her parents named her Grace when she was born in 1936. But that name was for a different kind of a girl, a lady, a delicate flower. She renamed herself as a teenager in the booming 1950s, running with a crowd of slick hair and rolled-up sleeves and mild larceny and mischief. The youngest child of three, the most rebellious, focused on fighting and fucking.

She lived hard, and became Kat, kicking off three generations of fast and loose and deeply wounded women.

There's the Grandma Kat I knew as a kid, in her forties and fifties—tough, a bit scary, bitter. Then there were stories I learned later: the time she had sex in the trunk of a car in the Fourth of July parade at the teeny age of fourteen. The multiple engagements she had as a teenager. The times she fended off my dad's dad.

And then there was her big project, something that still fascinates me. It's a Kat I recognize and don't.

In the 1980s, and then in the 1990s, Grandma Kat painstakingly assembled a family tree going back generations. Pre-internet, pre–23andMe spit tests and genetic reports on hair color and toe shape and behavioral tics, pre-Ancestry.com digital family trees, pre-podcasts of long-lost family secrets unearthed.

She went to the library, wrote letters to the National Genealogical Society, combed through microfiche and dusty rotting boxes. She collected photographs and records, whispers and rumors.

Where did she come from, and where did we come from, and where did this all start?

She talked about her project to her daughters and sons-in-law. No one cared, not in the face of everyday chaos, of feeding kids and putting on work clothes and navigating marriage and pushing down the feeling of disappointment, dissatisfaction, disgust, of *is this it, oh God this is it*.

But Kat kept working. There was something to find.

What was there to understand? What was Kat wishing to explain with her hunt for our names?

Perhaps it was pain.

I know facts about her life, from her, from her daughters. Facts conflated with myth and anger. And I know what I saw, and heard, and felt. I know myself. So I imagine.

After multiple teenage engagements, Kat found Carl, a short red-headed man who had driven a tank in Korea. She married him at eighteen. At nineteen, she had her first daughter. At twenty, she had her second. They all lived in a tiny house outside a small Iowa town.

Carl drove a long-haul truck, Kat stayed home. Long days and hours alone with her girls, waiting for him. And when he did get home, heat and fire: intense connection, followed by screaming fights. The girls outside, listening to their parents tear each other apart through the open windows. Occasionally, sounds of scuffle, of hands hitting flesh. Later, different sounds of bodies joining.

Carl also drove a motorcycle. And when Kat was thirty-six, Carl had a heart attack on that motorcycle. The crash was horrific, mythic. Stories from the daughters in later years would conflict and conflate—he was drinking, no he wasn't, he was with another woman, no he wasn't, he hit a semi, he just skidded out of control, his head was severed from his body, he looked fine. Kat never told stories.

Because then she was thirty-six and a widow, mother to two teenage girls. And what then?

Grandma Kat was often mean. I saw it, and heard stories, and put pieces together.

After their father's death, Kat abandoned her daughters in that moment of grief, abandoned her role as parent, froze them in trauma time.

The younger daughter, my Aunt Deb, gave up on school and started her lifelong search for her dead father in boyfriends and husbands. Across Nebraska, Minnesota, Montana; he was out there and she would find him.

The older daughter, my mother, Karen, she kept the house functioning. She intervened when her mother and sister tore at one another. She tried college for a few weeks, paid for by her father's friend. But she caved to a feeling of responsibility and pressure, the deep need from her mother and sister. She moved home and married the boy she was dating.

And Kat, I imagine she resented her daughters, their persistence at life, their moments of joy. Their worlds grown bigger. She, her world, tightened.

Just like my mom, Grandma Kat's anger came fast and furious, at unpredictable times. She scared her daughters and her grandkids. Her bite was something to avoid at all costs. That hand that held her cigarette, it had swollen knuckles and curled fingers, and the constant threat of a fist.

But she felt so deeply. Buried it, like all of us. Under a mask, under fierceness, brashness, fear.

Sometimes, though, she showed her feelings, laced with need.

When her mother got cancer from cigarettes, Kat brought her home. Ruth moved into that small house outside the city in 1992, at age eighty.

Before illness, Ruth wore great big glasses, blouses and slacks, pantyhose and open-toe sandals every day. She pinned her hair under a scarf every night. She had fake teeth. When we great-grandkids visited, she gave us outdoor tasks she'd designated for child labor that weekend, pointing with her long cigarette, her sandals' high heels digging into the grass.

She was the original source, the original model. She hid her anger under a well-heeled wardrobe and old age. But she was also widowed, and she'd scrounged and worked through the Depression, World War II, the tightening of gendered behaviors that came after. She survived, and she smoked, and made pan-fried hamburger patties, and gossiped with the rest of them. Like all the women in the family, she also had a fraught relationship with her daughter, full of unmet expectations, competitiveness, and wariness.

At Kat's house, Ruth loomed large, with oxygen tanks and beeping machines. But under all that she shrank. She gasped and sucked at air, and looked at her family with no recognition. Only pain.

Kat must have been crushed. This last effort to be valued, to be loved, and her mother didn't see her.

Kat kept working on the ancestry project after her mother died, until her own health started to fail. Her hands curled by arthritis, her breasts filled with masses, her lungs clouded with ash.

She was obsessed, possessed. More records, more photos. Time running out, little time left, to find the ties, to find the root. Her maternal family. Her paternal family. Her husband's family. Even her son-in-law's family. All of it, every detail. It would mean something. It would assemble into a whole.

She tracked down century-old lawmen on the prairie who gave us genes, a many-times-great-grandfather born on a boat fleeing Prussia in the 1850s, an entire lineage of farmers in France in the 1740s. A long line drawing us back to the Irish of the 1840s, driven out of their country by famine.

This, her records seem to say. This was noble. Myth-making tales that showed we were part of a bigger narrative. Better.

And maybe, it showed we were connected. We could connect. Even if we couldn't communicate.

After Grandma Kat died, my mom cleaned out her house. She collected all the worksheets into boxes and never looked at them.

One day I remembered a stray comment, a story about an ancestor born on a ship. I found the boxes, no small feat since my mother and I were rarely talking, the ancestry of genes and behavior passed down. I found Kat's work. And I understood, the need to hunt, the need to unearth, the need to explain, justify, validate. Why are we the way we are? Why are we trash, why are we mean, why are we alone, why are we bad? Why is this it?

And here, in Kat's work, there are lines, there are arrows back in time. A lineage, a map to righteous anger.

Look, Kat said through her letters and photos and names. Look at our family. Look at the misery that came before us. The times we had to run, and fight, and die. This is why we hurt.

This story is my story too, her search said.

But also, look at the persistence. Look, look at how we persevere. That's something. That's what we pass on.

I kept copies of Grandma Kat's work. The results, the charts and trees Kat created, they're impressive, yes. But more so is the act of searching. The diligence, the persistence. The decades-long quest to find an explanation for names, for why we're called names, why we must rename ourselves.

Years later, I stumbled on my own quest. I found a name for myself that I wasn't even looking for. And in that name, this genealogical hunt of Kat's looks different.

Kat searched for familial worth, a proof of connection, and a root of our pain. But maybe she was looking in the wrong place. Rather than assembling the seeds and branches of trees heavy with long-dead people, maybe she should have been looking for an idea, an abstract term that describes biology. A name for the way our brains work, and how that's different from other people.

She wouldn't have wanted this name. Her views on disability and difference were clear—something to be ridiculed, pitied. But it might have been her name just the same.

Kat was alive to see her granddaughter, me, pass the tender age of eighteen, twenty, twenty-five, without marrying. She was alive to hear me eschew marriage and kids.

How did this affect her search? Did she feel justified in her hunt, knowing that we were the last of this long maternal line? Did she hate me, resent my defiance of the rules?

Maybe Kat allowed herself a breath of relief. All the women on her charts and trees. All of them, all through time, birthing babies into this life. Just animals, rutting and dying. Because there was nothing else for it, nothing else for women to do. Look at them, all the women, in all the families, pushing the next generation out of their bodies, babies who would turn into teenage girls and then women who would be called trash, sluts, bitches. For reasons we never understood, but tried to accept anyway.

And maybe, this girl, this strange granddaughter doing things different, maybe she had paid attention. Watched Kat's quest. Listened to what was said and what wasn't.

I'd seen and heard what becomes of us. And I'd made a decision to end it.

Did Kat find sadness in this? Or hope?

## *III*

And what can you say about Aunt Deb?

Remember that time? Remember that other one?

Remember the dirty jokes, the tales of sex and drugs? The veneer of intimacy by sharing the taboo?

Remember her body? So out of control, fat to skinny, pretty to ugly, back and forth?

Remember all the stories she told, and we retold, as lesson, as reminder, as specter?

Remember the men?

*Carl*

Her first man is her father. He's the source of the red hair she and her older sister have. He's the source of family income. He's a force. He breaks up the fights between the sisters, between the sisters and their mother. Or he eggs them on. His anger, his hold on life, his hold on them.

He dies when Deb is fifteen, with such violence the family of women left behind can never sleep the night through.

Kat is broken, lost in her own grief and rage. Karen is determined to keep the mechanics of life moving. And Deborah, the third? The youngest? She sees no safety without men. No love or cohesion. She will remember this.

*Mark 1*

Deb is smart—she skips a grade, has big potential. But it's 1975, and she's a girl. What can she really do?

Mark is there, and he's decent, and he wants her. She wants to be wanted. She wants to be seen. She wants something of her own. Something stable. A man to protect her and love her, like her dad did. Or at least, her scrubbed-clean memories of her dad. The memories of life before his death.

She's eighteen and gets married. Just like her sister. Just like her mom. Just like her grandma. Following the lead. What else do you do?

She plays the part for a while. But then something, some spark, some bit of anger at this, her life mapped out at eighteen, a life that had so much potential, it ignites.

So she's the first of the long line of women before her to leave a husband of her own volition.

This is the first of many reasons she will be the secret butt of jokes, the pitied and pitiable one, the punching bag for a family who needs one.

*Carl*

Deb probably remembers him as she moves to another town, tries on a new life. She probably likes to think he's a little proud of her. Sure, she's bucking the system, and he had a rule-following army side to him that would frown on that. But he also had a hellraiser side to him. And look at his little firecracker. She's going to do things her own way.

By now Karen has a kid. Another little redheaded girl. Deb visits her niece and looks at that girl, looks at the family surrounding her, looks at the baby-faced mother and the young grandmother, the child of a dad. None of them, not one, knows what they're doing.

(She looks at little me, and maybe it's then that Deb decides: she won't pass this on.)

*Unnamed*

She meets another guy, and she can't help it. She dreams of the kind of love she's mythologized. She dreams of being seen, being connected.

It doesn't matter what his name is. That detail has been lost to time, to strained family relations, to a deliberate burial.

Deb falls for this man. It's still the 1970s, and she's still so young, so forgive her if she doesn't see the signs. Others won't forgive her; they'll chalk it up to her bad luck, they'll think it's her punishment for leaving the first one. For thinking she was too good for a decent, normal guy.

So this one, this unnamed man shape, he doesn't fully show himself until after they're married. That's when he hits her.

Forgive her too, for being disappointed, but not surprised. Because her father and her mother, they fought. She and her sister, outside the house, hearing sounds of flesh hitting other flesh. Whether it was violence or sex, don't they both show love?

Who knows how long it goes on, how long Deb keeps herself there. Maybe she's ashamed—it's bad enough to leave one husband, but two? Maybe she deserves this.

*Tom*

Until one night this unnamed husband hits and hits, and Deb is knocked out of her shame and stasis, knocked into fight or flight.

She flees to the house where her sister lives, along with her tiny niece, and her brother-in-law, Tom, the newly minted policeman.

Deb's crying, look at her, and her face, look, it shows the purple-blue marks of truth, the thing everyone has suspected but no one talks about.

And Tom, he answers the door, comes outside, alert and ready. Because here comes another car, the no-name husband, still swollen with anger and righteousness, screeching down the street, barreling out of the car, onto the lawn, toward the door, demanding the return of his property.

Tom, what does he think? With his new job, he's infused with purpose, justice manifest, the law embodied. And women—Tom knows you can fuck around on them, and you can belittle them, and you can make a stink when one is assigned as your partner, and you can view them as less than. But you can't hit them.

So he extends an arm into a straight clothesline and knocks the husband off his feet.

*Carl*

In the past, this wouldn't have been a reason to leave. But it's the 1980s now. And Deb feels power in others knowing the truth as she files for divorce again.

She has her dad watching over her. She believes this.

And Karen, she learns from this moment too. Here Tom was, protecting them. Like Carl had. So Karen can put up with her husband's affairs, right? She can learn to live with disappointment. In fact, she'll recommit. Work harder. Have another baby. Or twins, as it turns out. They'll be happy, and she will be safe.

She'll never be alone. Not like Deb.

*Mark 2*

And now we come to the time the niece starts to form memories. She will remember the aunt most vividly in this moment in time, these costumes, this version.

(Later, I'll repeat the family's pattern. I'll tell stories of my wild, crazy aunt for laughs. I'll make fun of her to other family members. Later still I'll be haunted and ashamed by this).

But right now it's the mid-1980s, so picture this for Deb: wild, huge, hot-rolled red hair. Thin yet buxom body. Leather clad. A biker chick, old lady to husband number three.

And he, this husband, he has the name of the normal, boring guy from the past. But this Mark rides loud motorcycles and works on vintage bikes and cars, and breeds wolves in a trailer park outside the city.

Deb and Mark form a wild, scary alter image to the niece's parents, the bank teller and the cop. When the couple arrive somewhere in a blur, the energy turns frantic and frenetic. Tom knows cocaine and meth fuel this shift; the niece will learn all this later. But even then, without that element of knowledge, the stories come fast, the legends form instantaneously.

Remember the time, the niece will say long into adult life to her brothers, knowing they were too young but willing them to share her memory. Remember? That one Christmas, maybe '85 or '86? When Aunt Deb showed up with a boob job? And gave us all ornately framed photos of herself in a black teddy? And Grandma Kat hung hers on her wall for the rest of her life?

During this time there is also talk of Deb's other surgery, the tying of tubes. It's not a phase like some thought. She's really not going to have kids. Imagine that. Women without kids.

Now, the niece. She doesn't know what tubes are, or how tying them ensures no babies. But there's something inside her, a thrum beat of recognition, a wild sense of freedom. Because she's nine and ten and eleven, learning about how her body will change, experiencing bleeding without dying, and feeling a deep guttural fear at what she is capable of. A terror, so young, of being wanted by men. Of being a mother someday. Soon, in fact.

Karen talks about Deb with disdain—she's bored so easily, she's so immature, she doesn't live in the real world, who does she think she is.

(I only feel my curiosity grow.)

*Carl*

But here's the thing.

Deb tied her tubes, and she cut off a lineage.

In this family, you're a kid, then you're a teen, one who resents your mother. Then you get married, and then you're a mom. And only in that way do you understand your own mother.

Deb and her mother always fought, but especially after Carl's death. Without him around to break up the fights, they continued. Without completing the pattern, without Deb having her own children, they never came to truly understand one another.

They were just two women, and women in this family never truly connect. Women must compete with one another. Especially over men.

Remember, the niece and nephews will say as adults. Remember when we figured out Grandma Kat fucked Mark 2?

They'll wonder who had him first. They'll wonder which order was better.

(I'll learn he wasn't the only one.)

*Rich*

Why Deb and Mark 2 split, the niece doesn't know. Maybe because Deb was arrested with her fanny pack of crystal meth. Maybe because they were high all the time, so the highs got harder to achieve and lows harder to escape. Maybe because he fucked her mom.

Whatever happens, they split, and she leaves town.

When Aunt Deb shows up again, it's the 1990s. And she's a new person.

Khakis. Neatly coiffed hair. Button-down shirts covering her purchased chest. She's accompanied by a lawyer, a professional man, a moneyed man. Bald, glasses, fat. He talks about mortgages and investments. He golfs in his free time. So she does too.

Is this Deb? Can it be? She was so bold, so wild. And sure, she still cusses with every breath and still tells dick jokes. But she's so . . . constrained? Limited?

Among the family, the stories about Deb shift. Here she is, they say, playing at respectability. But we'll take it. As boring as Rich is, he's predictable. She's predictable.

Her body, though. This is when it becomes big, bigger, bigger still. And that may be a more significant sacrilege than all her past behavior. She's fat, and fat is the worst you can be.

And just like with every husband, there's the initial heat and consummation, followed by the long decline. She's sought a partner—a lover but also a confidante. A friend. And it's failed, again.

At some point, Deb is so lonely, so alone, she confides in her sister. Yes, it's a mistake. Everyone knows you cannot be vulnerable with each other in this family, especially the women. They know it will be spread, stretched, used for manipulation. But in all her years of chasing connection through men, Deb never made girlfriends. Never trusted other women. Why would she, when she can't trust her own sister, her own mom?

But desperation. Sadness. Loneliness. Deb tells her sister that Rich won't fuck her, disgusted with their mutual fatness.

This is a choice tidbit, a validation of the family's gleeful disgust in Deb's body. Karen tells her husband, her teenage daughter, her mother, her friends. She uses it to justify her own horrific fear of her body, to teach her daughter to fear hers.

Maybe Deb knows everyone whispers about her; maybe she catches them. Maybe she chooses to believe her family wants the best for her. Maybe in the middle of all the golf, the outfits and the irons and the rules, she remembers riding a motorcycle down interstates. She remembers the howl of those wolves. Maybe without sex, her tool to trap, she's at a loss. Maybe Carl talks to her, and she talks to him.

You know what happens next.

*Tom*

Maybe Deb feels emboldened this time. Because Karen, the good daughter, her perfect sister with the perfect family, she cheats on her husband and blows up their marriage. Or he cheats on her (again) and blows up the marriage. Or both. The stories conflict. The situation remains. A twenty-six-year marriage gone.

The niece, she's out of college now, living in Chicago. She's fielding calls and visits from both parents, being swayed to their sides. Just like when she was a young girl, told her parents' problems as a tiny confidante, pushed into parenting her brothers and her parents. The adults in her life, they are childish, sniping at one another, fighting in public.

(I've learned: no one grew up in my family. No one learned how.)

So this time, when Deb divorces husband four, it's not the biggest news, the biggest drama, the content of whispers and gleeful mocking. Everyone has shown themselves.

Deb should feel happy. Justified.

But that idea, that hope, that dream of being loved again, being seen. No other woman can see her. So a man it must be.

*Mark 3*

We're in the 2000s now, so Deb goes online. She's starved herself for a while. She's flush with alimony cash. She's ready to play the game.

The family learns she's married again from a holiday card, the return address with a new last name.

This Mark: as if someone took all the past husbands and blended them, the result a chalky, grainy mess that parches the throat and gums the teeth. He's in Montana, a house in the middle of nowhere. He's a survivalist. All the makings of a murder documentary or a cult docuseries.

Does the idea of survival appeal to her? She's made it decades now as a broken, bleeding thing, and she's lived through it. She's tougher than the dumbfucks around her. She's known for baring her teeth. So yeah, she understands this Mark, who says the government is out to fuck them all over, that society will break down. His cabin is filled with guns and meth and the idea of outlasting the rest of the world.

And maybe the idea of the two of them together, against the world—maybe it promises true connection. Someone to talk to.

She disappears into the wilderness.

*Carl*

When Grandma Kat dies, the family gathers in cars on rural Iowa highways, driving to small town cemeteries to split Kat's ashes among her parents' and husband's gravesides.

Deb and Mark 3 show up high. As Karen pours bits of burned bone and blood onto graves, this couple cackles, spouts Jimi Hendrix facts, tells stories about anal sex.

Suppose there is an afterlife. Suppose Carl and Kat are reunited on this day, and they look down from a cloudy heaven to their daughters. They see Deb and the latest man, perhaps the worst. And they see Karen and her new husband, a blustering bully.

In another family, these ghostly parents might reach for their girls, try to heal the gaping wounds under the skin, the festering sores that make them grab onto mean men.

But in this family, Carl and Kat tore at one another while alive, sliced the first cuts inside their girls. They have no perception beyond their own grasping, suffocating love. They have nothing to give their girls, then or now.

So Karen and Deb cling to their twisted love and mean men, sneer at each other, and feel utterly alone.

*Michael*

Meanwhile, the niece believes she's stopped the bleeding. She's in her twenties now, and has not become a teen mother or a divorcee. She's declared her intention never to wed, never to have children. She knows she must protect herself, must never mold herself to the man, not like her aunt and mother do.

She believes she's chosen a man who respects her, who truly loves her, who would never hurt her.

She believes she is different.

(I have much learning to do.)

*All*

Deb is in Montana, and Mark 3 has burned through her thousands and thousands of dollars in alimony, and they're surviving, yes, and together, and . . .

So fucking alone. Always, so alone. The worst kind of alone, when a man is next to you in bed and you should not feel alone.

This feeling. If only she could talk to her sister about it. They both understand this pit of particular loneliness. So does Deb's niece, a woman now, living with her own man, starting to understand.

Why can't they talk? Why can't they come together as women of this line, of a long lineage of women so alone in their own skin?

There's a disconnect, in their brains and biology, and a lesson handed down over that vast genealogical tree. And it breaks them, again and again.

*Carl*

Deb's nephews are men now. Does that passage of time, that circularity, speak to her?

Whatever does it this time, when she divorces her fifth husband, broke and high and desperate, her nephews are men with trucks and strong arms. They help her move home, into a small apartment in Iowa.

And maybe this time, she can be happy with that. Knowing there are men of her own blood nearby, two boys that, in the right light, look like her dad.

*Men on Apps*

It's the 2010s now, and dating is transformed.

Because she can't not. She can't be alone. It's just been days, months since her worst divorce yet, and the silence around her and the screaming in her head will not let her be.

It's all she thinks about. All she talks about. Without a man in her life she doesn't know what to think, what to do, who to be. But the men now—they're so old! Yes, she's in her midfifties. But she's attracted to youth. To virility. To a moment frozen in time. These men are all older than her father ever got to be. They're all aged and stooped under their baggage. Is this what she has to work with now?

Fine. So be it. She will fuck old men. It's better than that quiet apartment.

They're on the path to marriage. Her sixth. But this one—it's real love, she says. True love. What she's been looking for.

He's retired from something lucrative. He spends thousands building model planes that fly at regional events. He buys her elaborate heels for sexual role-play, which they then nail to the wall as art.

So she's in her sixties, and has this boyfriend, and maybe this will be it. Maybe this time.

Maybe, in the least, she can find a stasis. She can embrace his passions as her own once more, telling her uninterested family about the ins and outs of small airplanes. She can tell her dirty jokes and share stories of their sex wall with the family. She can find a way to live with the disappointment that inevitably arrives. She can find a way to live with the refrain of despair in their shared bed. She can convince herself that he loves her as she needs.

(Maybe.)

What can you say about Aunt Deb? She's left five terrible husbands. She's been different in a time that didn't want her to be. Remember that time? Remember that other one? She's believed what other people have told her, about her body, her mind, her heart. She can be cruel and capricious, like her mother and sister.

She is often in pain, and punching down. She has been living unmoored. Unnamed. Unrecognizable.

But she's always trying to find her way to something better. To someone who will show connection is possible.

Remember? The men? So many of them. And she keeps going, keeps trying. Because what else is there?

## *IV*

Let's play a game! It's simple, really. See, there's this deck of cards, and within the deck even numbers are worth ten points and odd numbers are worth five, and the suits of the cards, well, that's a range of values too. You start with the person on your right, and you have to watch what they put down, and oh right, the aces are the worst, and the queens get the most. And oh yeah, a few more things . . .

Don't cry. Don't panic. See, it's funny, it's fine, they're joking, they're saying it again, *Amy is so smart, but so dumb with games, it's hilarious.* And it is funny, how afraid I am of these games, how my brain stops working and goes black. They're just games, it doesn't matter who wins or loses, it doesn't matter if I mess up or break the rules.

Don't think about my family. How Mom loves games, and is always trying to get me to play, is so annoyed when I won't. Why can't I just be what she wants? Games are just fun, they're just what normal people do. Calm down. You're being too weird.

Too late. I hear her voice in my head.

Let's play this board game! You're gonna love it. Okay, so, you get all these playing pieces, and your goal is to build something, a farm or a property or a space station, and to take something from your opponents, but every roll of the dice is coded, and you need the instruction manual to tell you what to do, but it's so easy, and so fun, let's start, you'll get the hang of it . . .

Oh Amy, I've been looking forward to this trip. I look forward to these weekends away, without your dad, just you and me and your little brothers at your great-grandma's house. I'm sure Grandma Ruth has some house tasks you can work on, some chores to finish, while she and I talk. Cuz she just gets me. No one else gets me.

I love when you and I can just talk here in the car too. Because I need to talk to someone. Work, you know, they just don't appreciate how much I do. Your dad, he doesn't appreciate how much I do. The stress, all of it, all the things I have to do for you kids because no one else will. And then I'm eating too much, and I'm going to get gross and fat, with my thighs rubbing together. I don't have anyone to talk to now; what will happen if I get ugly? It's all too much.

You're eight now, and everything is just so easy for you. But you'll see.

What'd you say? Don't say that. Don't do that. I said *don't*. Don't you dare. Why aren't you wearing a skirt? You know the rules. I don't want you to look like a boy. What'd you do to your hair? Why are you eating that? Make some effort.

You think this is yelling? This is nothing. You think I'm a bad mom? I love you unconditionally. Not like my mom.

Shut up—just let me cry. You don't have to fix everything. That's not what friends do.

All I wanted is for you to be my friend.

Wipe that look off your face.

Let's play another game! It's like Charades, except you have to use a prop to help you act out the word, and you can only use one prop at a time, and can't use one you've already used, and can't have it be, like, the actual clue, and yes, you're doing this all standing up, in front of the group, and we're looking at you and guessing and laughing with you (and also at you), and, okay, here we go!

Friendship is a losing game, honey. See, friends will leave you, and make fun of you, because they're girls. We can't be friends with other women, it just won't work. Too much competition, too much cattiness. That's why your friends dumped you.

You're eleven, you'll get over it.

Oh, okay, so you want help. I know—confront them. Ask them if you stink or something. Everyone loves when you make fun of yourself. What? I'm just trying to help. They said you gossiped about the fat girl? I mean, everyone does. Who do they think they are? I gossip too—that's just the game. And then suddenly someone says that's bad? It makes no sense.

That's why friends don't, won't understand you. That's why you and I have to stick together. You're my world. Without you, I don't know what I'd do.

Why are you pulling away like that? Why are you so sour? Get out of your bad mood. You have nothing to be mad about, or sad about.

What'd you say? What big word are you using? What, are you trying to embarrass me? You think you're better than me?

Yeah, I used to think my mom was a dumb bitch too. Then I had you.

## Let's play Jenga! Balance, and risk, and public shaming—it's perfect!

So you were in talented and gifted in elementary school. And yes, all your seventh grade report cards are filled with As. And yes, you're twelve years old and reading all those history books and the daily newspaper, spouting all those facts about the Russians, the Holocaust, Egyptian and Greek myths, the nuclear bomb, on and on. And yes, you got one of the highest scores in the city on the Iowa Test of Basic Skills.

But you really want to go to a separate school for half the day to take college classes? For the next five years? With kids from all the other city schools? Why?

You know those kids will be kind of weird, right? And they'll be from the other sides of town, with more money. They'll have things you won't have. You sure you want to be around them?

Look at you, thinking this will get you somewhere.

Well, it's free, and you can ride the city bus there. So sure. Knock yourself out.

## Let's play Operation!

Women don't understand us. And men, they just want things.

Listen, you're fourteen, you need to know this. Your dad, well, he pushed me, okay? I was fifteen, and he was seventeen, and he wanted the thing all men want, and he told me if I didn't give it up, he'd move on. And he was the quarterback, the captain, the star. His family already thought my mom was trash, and we were trash. They told him he should go after someone else. And look, sex wasn't great, and it hurt, but it made him happy for a while.

Did I ever tell you how he kissed my cousin on our wedding day? Did I ever tell you about the time he flirted with your Aunt Deb? Did I ever tell you about the affairs he had when you were little? Did I ever tell you that I stayed with him because he's a good dad? That I stayed because of you?

Get that look off your face. Jesus. I'm just being honest. That's what you want, right? You're supposed to be my friend. Come on, let's go get Glamour Shots. You'll feel better when you look prettier. Then we'll get Dairy Queen. I know it's bad, and I know we should lose some weight, but it'll be our secret. Ours alone.

Let's play Hearts!

Sure, you're seventeen, and you took all those college classes, and you were valedictorian, and you've accumulated a ton of scholarships, and you've been working toward this for years.

But if you go to college, who will I talk to?

I'll visit on weekends and we can go to the bars together! Won't that be fun? We'll drink, and flirt with guys, and I can catch you up on what you're missing at home.

No? You have to study? You're underage? You want to spend weekends with your boyfriend? You're so selfish. I never got to do this, you know.

And you had sex with your boyfriend? What a slut. I obviously can't trust you.

Why don't you tell me things? Why do you pull away? I love you unconditionally, don't you see that?

Let's play Go Fish!

Here we are. Your aunt and her fourth husband and me. We showed up, here to your fancy Phi Beta Kappa ceremony in this gaudy college auditorium. Drove the hours here, sitting in the front row; let's see you get this award.

Oh there's a speech first? Why is that ugly, frumpy woman talking about frogs? That's her research? Why? This is what happens at college?

The fuck is she doing, wasting time on this? Stupid bitch.

Yeah, we said that out loud, and said it too loud, and laughed, and the lady noticed, and the rest of the audience too. And you, up on the stage, turning red.

Who does that snooty cunt think she is? Who do you think you are?

Let's play Battleship!

If you move to Chicago, what am I supposed to do? Who will I talk to? What will I tell people—that you hate me so much you have to move six hours away?

So you're really going. Fine. Then I have to take you. We'll drive to Chicago this weekend.

Oh, and this guy from work will come along too.

Wasn't he great? Wasn't he funny? He's someone I can talk to, now that you're leaving.

Let's play Asshole!

Now that you're twenty-three, and your brothers are graduated from high school, your dad and I are getting a divorce.

We just grew apart, that's all. Nothing else to the story. No one else.

Let's play Sorry!

Just months later, and I find out your dad is dating my best friend? He fucked that cunt, and you're okay with that? Who are you loyal to? What kind of a bitch sides with him? There are absolutely sides. You are unbelievable. You're a slut, just like her.

My friend? The man from our Chicago trip? Leave him out of this.

Let's play Gin!

Your dad has someone. He has *her*. I have to have someone.

Yeah, he and I both got fired from our jobs for unhinged and drunken behavior. And we both got blackout drunk at your brother's wedding, and passed out in a car on the side of the road. And yeah, he hit me, and yeah, we got arrested in Vegas for fighting. But I gave as good as I got, so what's the big deal?

This is fire, this is love. Just like my mom and dad.

Yeah, I don't feel safe, but what are my options? My money is with him.

Without him, I'll be a fifty-year-old woman alone, and what then?

Wait, you'll let me stay with you? Okay, I'll leave him. I'll do it.

Let's play Candy Land!

We're engaged! Aren't you so happy for us? Why can't you be happy? What is wrong with you? Because I'm with him, I can buy things for you. What's the problem?

What are you talking about? I never said that. Never did that. You're making things up, like always.

You think you know things because you're in your thirties? You don't know shit. You don't know me.

You know what? Fine. Fuck you. We're done.

Let's play Sorry! again!

Three years, huh? That's how long it took you to say sorry. Three years of silence. Three years that I left you out of family events. Three years, and finally, you apologize.

What do I have to apologize for? I didn't do that. Didn't say that.

Yeah, I heard about your breakup from your ten-year unmarried relationship. So what? Why would I have broken this silence you caused to reach out to you?

And now look at you, moving back home from the big city. I won't say it looks like failure, but, you know.

Look, it's going to have to be different if you want me in your life. You're going to have to call me every week—I don't care that you hate the phone. And you're going to have to come on trips, up to our boat house—I don't care that you are terrified of boats. And you're going to have to defer to me on holidays—I don't care that they give you panic attacks. You're going to do what I say, because we don't want to go back to not talking, do we? We don't want the little ones, your nephews, to see how you hate the family, do we?

Also, you're going to be nice to him.

Let's play Old Maid!

You really stuck with it, didn't you? Being alone? Not having kids or getting married?

> You need to make more time for me. You need to make a better showing. You need to call him, and give him gifts, and treat him like a dad. You need to know better.
>
> You got a master's? You got another? You wrote a book? Oh. I could have done that too, if things were different.
>
> What do you mean I set you up to fail? What do you mean "that's mean"? You can't talk to me this way. You're too sensitive. Grow up. You wouldn't act like this if you were a mom.
>
> You can only understand and forgive your mother if you have kids of your own.

Let's play Memory!

> I mean, is this "pandemic" really real? I don't know anyone who has it. And masks, come on. Okay, libs, you want to control me? Then tell us the truth about the election. Tell us how you stole it from Trump.
>
> You're not coming to Christmas? It's just twenty people. All my good God-fearing in-laws. Plus your brothers and their families. Testing? Masks? What the fuck? Jesus Christ. You put all this nonsense above your family?
>
> Do you do this with your dad? Oh, he canceled Christmas? Just with you kids, though, right? He kept a holiday with his wife and stepdaughter? Shows his priorities.
>
> You're not a good daughter. That's it. Back to silence we go.
>
> I love you unconditionally, and once you realize that, that I'm the only one who does, you'll come back.
>
> This is your fault.

Let's play a game! Let's go around the table and say how much we love our moms. Let's say the best thing you've done with your mom. Let's talk about Mother's Day plans. Let's talk about how we should call our moms. Let's talk about how our moms know us best. Let's talk about forgiveness and grace. Let's talk about being less selfish and self-absorbed, and just loving your mom with all her flaws. Let's talk about doing the right thing and putting your mom first.

I will not panic. It's dumb to panic. I *am* being too sensitive. It's just a game. I'm used to games. I was raised with games. I learned how to play games by example and by pain and by fear. I learned how no one else will help you with a game. I learned how the players will deny that you are playing a game. I learned it matters more than anything that the other player must always win. I learned that the winning player holds all the cards and will not let me play any more games until I admit defeat. I learned it's normal to play these games. I learned that all relationships are games.

Let's play a game?

I'll have to play Sorry! again. I'll have to prostrate myself, admit all fault, I'll have to never mention anything about public health, and the news, and bisexuality, and autism, if I want to be allowed back in. If I'm to be included in family events, if I'm to be acknowledged. If I want to be loved. In the meantime, it's silence.

My brothers hear the stories she tells about me, and it's just easier to fall in line. They distance themselves from me. My dad does nothing.

I'm sad. I'm ashamed. But I'm also tired. Exhausted from games. I finally understand why I hate games, and why she and I will never coexist without the game. So what's the point in playing?

I won't play. I'll be the bad daughter, the terrible, horrible, no-good, very-bad daughter who protects herself. Who cuts her mother out of her life. I'll stop reacting and take action. I'll put games aside for good. And what comes will come.

## *V*

### *Multiplicity*

Mothers are set up to fail. American mothers especially, midwestern mothers, told to do their duty and do it alone and do it without support and do it well, and don't complain, what are you complaining about, everyone does it, everyone must do it, you're not special, you're not believable.

So the women and mothers in my family, they did what they were supposed to do, and they did the best they could, and they failed.

*Singularity*

I failed too, as a sensitive kid asked to do too much. I failed as a smug young adult, thinking I would do better by making different choices. I failed as a suicidal middle-aged woman who never asked myself the right questions.

*Multiplicity*

If there are indeed multiple worlds, multiple parallel realities where the decisions we make create different heres and nows, then I would have made different choices. Maybe I would have had kids. And maybe that would have solved the issue of being able to talk to my family.

*Singularity*

I never wanted kids. Chalk it up to babysitting my twin brothers while I was in elementary school. Or to being farmed out as childcare around the neighborhood when I was in junior high. Blame it on being a parent to my mom and dad, leaning on me as a mini adult, a nine-year-old wise woman. Blame it on closely watching the lives of Grandma Kat and Aunt Deb and my mom.

By the time I was in high school, I was tired of being a parent to children and adults, and to myself. And I knew I'd already fucked up. The pressure and games and hardness I had learned, I'd passed it down to my brothers. At ten years old, responsible for taking care of five-year-old twins, I told them toxic fairy tales of my own creation, full of violence and bulimic princesses and bad guys winning the day. I told them the stories I was hearing about what would happen to their bodies and what sex was, when they were still in preschool. I ruined holidays for them by revealing the lie of Santa. I was a kid, frustrated at being a parent, and I took it out on them. Just like my parents, and their parents, and back and back.

So by college I knew I would never have kids. As I grew older, left home, and my parents repeatedly called me to parent my brothers—to fix issues, to pass on messages, to be the final say—my resolve grew.

By the time I was an adult, I knew I could barely take care of myself. Why would I pass my deep confusion and pain to someone else, give my childhood and adulthood depression and anxiety and panic to another young girl? Why bring someone else into this mess?

*Multiplicity*

I'm incredibly lucky because that resolve stood. For all the sex I've had, I never got pregnant, never even had a scare. Maybe I'm sterile. Maybe the pills and patches and shots and devices did their job. Maybe the timing just worked.

Whatever the ultimate reason, if I had gotten pregnant, I would have gotten an abortion, gotten another. And I had the capability for that, my baby-making years coinciding with legality. I'm lucky. I could make my desire reality.

In other worlds, it's different. And here, now, in the United States, it's different. So many other possibilities, terrible and wondrous.

*Singularity*

When I was in my twenties, and people asked when I was going to marry and have kids, because you can apparently ask women anything, I told them about my lack of plans for either, and they chuckled, or cocked their head, or put a hand on my shoulder, or smirked. "You'll change your mind."

When I was in my thirties, and people asked about my husband, because people continued to be nosy motherfuckers, I affirmed my lack of plans for a man or babies, and they blanched. Their foreheads crumpled. Their breath stopped short at my selfishness. "You'll regret it."

In my forties, and people are still asking where my husband is, or how many kids I have. Men in my house fixing things, asking why I live in this house all on my own. My tubes clipped tight against eggs and the flames of perimenopause sparking, and they're so sad for me, rush to think of something, anything else to ask a woman. "How many cats do you have?"

*Multiplicity*

In other worlds, maybe female bodies aren't expected to cede to male bodies at all times. They're not worth less than a man's, in sports, at work, in a marriage, in courts. Female bodies that are not white are also not considered inherently less. Bodies that are not small and trim still count. Bodies and minds, even if they're made different, are valued. Maybe we don't need anger, and it doesn't tear us apart.

*Singularity*

In this world no one told me how to be an adult. Because no one in my family knew. No one taught how to love, and how to earn love, and how to spot abuse masquerading as love. How to value bodies. How to believe truths and spot lies. Because they didn't know.

No one taught me how to be different, how to be odd, to bear the weight of what I didn't do. Because it was easier to just do it the way it's been done before.

*Multiplicity*

Maybe in another world, I have kids, and I cling to my mother for her knowledge, and appreciate my father for his hardness. I commiserate with my brothers as they create their families and we grow closer for it. Maybe that's how we talk.

Maybe in another world, I give in to my homesickness my first semester of college, cede to the guilt of leaving my mom, to the confusion and frustration I feel as the only one in my family to leave. In that world, I come home, and stay home, as my parents had, as they secretly want me to. I come home, and stay home, and don't live in a big city, don't travel, don't meet people. So I can be like them. In that way, maybe, they like me.

In another world, they understand words. They know what "unconditional" means. So I know my worth.

In another world, I'm not a slut. In another world, I'm not a depressed panic-driven live wire. In another world, I'm still with the dangerous ex-boyfriend, compliant and complicit. In another world, I'm still starving myself, poisoning my insides, breaking my body. In another world, I don't become vegan, a laughable travesty in meat and potato land, who is ignored at every family dinner. In another world, I keep my queerness quiet. And by doing or not doing these things, I keep my connection to my family.

In another world, I never find out I am autistic. I never start putting pieces together, for myself and my family, never ask the questions that start this whole fucking thing. I never look at our failure to communicate, to connect, our inability and refusal, as something that's part of our animal blood.

None of those things happened. So maybe we talk. We are in pain, maybe. But we're in pain together.

*Singularity*

If other realities exist, I grieve them. I grieve that I don't live in a world where my family can talk, actually support one another, actually know one another. I grieve that I don't live in a world where I knew some of my difference was biology, where I could understand myself and my struggles as autistic. I grieve that I don't live in a world where I knew my worth early on, and never begged and pleaded my family to recognize it.

I grieve, but also cheer for those other Amys.

# Part 3 Bad Woman

# Slut, Slattern, Spinster: A Gallery

TITLE: Slut

ART DESCRIPTION: A black-and-white silhouette of a female figure bent over a piece of lined notebook paper, pen in hand. Names are listed on the paper.

PLACARD NOTES: I don't remember most of my sexual encounters. Sex with people I dated and sex with random dalliances—I only remember flashes of some, big black spots of emptiness with others. I've forgotten what some partners look like, what their names are.

A good portion of my sex has been hidden by the dissociative properties of the brain, protecting me from remembering humiliation and confusion. The embarrassments of high school baby steps, the mortifications of college mean boys or clingy boys or sick boys, the exhaustion and blurred lines of angry men and desperate men and disappointing men.

Another sizable portion of my sex has been forgotten because it was forgettable. Hours spent trying to resuscitate whiskey dick. Hours spent trying to come for persistent girls. Hours spent trying not to laugh, to fart, to queef, to puke; hours spent trying to look sexy, whatever that means. Hours bombed out of my mind, fucking to feel.

This is a shameful confession, right? A slut's gallery—who wants to see that?

TITLE: Whore

ART DESCRIPTION: A pencil drawing of a man watching a pornographic video and taking notes.

PLACARD NOTES: *Can I fuck you?* the Choker asked. He sat across from me at a bar in an ill-fitting suit. Since I'd had multiple beers and months of solo sex, I agreed.

But as soon as we were in my bedroom, clothes coming off, I wanted him gone. I already knew I was not interested in seeing him again, already knew this would be a lackluster endeavor. I could have said I changed my mind. Told a lie or told the truth. But as usual, I thought of politeness, of being seen as a tease. I thought of hurt feelings, and how men with hurt feelings can lash out. So I fucked him.

I turned it into a joke afterward with friends: how the sex was so bland I forgot I'd had it. How he kept saying what he would do to me and wouldn't actually do it. How he choked me, and told me how much I liked it.

I didn't tell my friends how he moved me around like a posable bot, how he talked to himself more than me, how he said he'd wear a condom and then didn't, how I smiled when he choked me so I could remind him I was alive.

TITLE: Minx

ART DESCRIPTION: Cubist style; male shape between a female shape's legs.

PLACARD NOTES: *Tell me what you like*, the Nice Guy said. His face smeared with me. His hair wet with sweat. His fingers moving down to replace his tongue.

A simple question, one the man wants answered simply. Put your tongue here. Move it faster. Or slower. Push deeper with your fingers. Yes. There. Right there. He wants a button to push, an equation to which he can apply a formula.

All while I'm watching the clock on the wall or in my head. I'm taking too long. I need to come faster. He's going to tire. He's going to get frustrated. He's going to get annoyed.

*Tell me what you like.*

And my mind goes blank.

Because what I truly like is the illusion of release, and the idea of connection. I like it most when someone likes me, likes to touch me.

And the rest is an empty space, waiting to be filled. That's what they're supposed to do: fill that hole. Pour themselves into it, make me what they want. Make me into a mirror. Make me whole.

TITLE: Harlot

ART DESCRIPTION: A screenshot of the stepmother's penis wall from *Fleabag*.

PLACARD NOTES: The Soft Dick. The Small Dick. The Poly Guy. The Hot Mess. The Less Hot Mess. The Redhead. The Nerd. The Pegging Guy. The Scared Girl. The "We Belong Together" Girl. The Greek Guy, the Thai Guy, the Indian Guy, the Lebanese Guy, the Russian Guy, the Russian Girl, the South African Guy, the South African Girl. The Chicago Club Guys and Girls. The Scary Guys. The Angry Guys. The Desperate Guys. The Hopeful Girls. And on and on.

Should I be ashamed of this (incomplete) (vague) (sort of depressing) list? Should I be proud?

With each person, I'm swept up in what they say, what they do. I'm swept up by their image of me, an image I project knowingly and unknowingly. I'm swept up by the idea of them, the idea of me, the idea of us. That sweeping can last as long as a few minutes, or a few months, or many years. That sweeping always ends.

TITLE: Bimbo

ART DESCRIPTION: A digital sign, with numbers advancing on a set rhythm.

PLACARD NOTES: When does a slut become a slut?

Is there a numeral that achieves it? Is it more than one? A handful? Double digits?

Is it a combination of age and numbers? X + Y = Z; a girl's age plus the number of partners = slut?

Do you have to be hot to be a slut? Does hotness change the term to bimbo? And what is the physical criteria for hot?

I'm middle-aged and still don't know the full answers to these questions.

But I do know:

A slut has sex.

A slut is rumored to have sex.

A slut is unmarried.

A slut may become married, and through marriage transform out of sluthood, but the specter of her slutty past remains, and will be used for shame if the marriage fails.

A slut is a woman who has sex without the explicit intention to procreate.

A slut is a woman.

TITLE: Tramp

ART DESCRIPTION: A slideshow of red As, in different fonts, different sizes, different art treatments.

PLACARD NOTES: Another known idea: having sex with a partnered person makes you a slut. Of course, this only applies to the female in the formula; the man does not earn such a name. Adultery falls on the woman, and falls hard. I had sex with people when I was partnered and they were married, and that fact alone wipes away differential calculations of numbers and age, and lands firmly in the category of slut. No matter if feelings were involved, love even; no matter if the people we cheated on didn't see us and even hurt us. Life for women is rules, and this is a hard and fast one: thou shalt not commit adultery, or covet, or fuck beyond the bounds of your legal sex.

TITLE: Dyke

ART DESCRIPTION: Three watercolor outlines of women, limbs entwined on a rectangular form.

PLACARD NOTES: Sex is over when the man is spent. His dick empty, the contents evident on his body or mine or on the sheets. His body at rest.

When I had sex with women for the first time, there was no ending. No evidence. We just kept going.

There was a moment, in an apartment, the three of us listening to music, when we were all girl beings for whom sex was mostly a probing, a penetration, a ride where our pleasure was mostly optional. The majority of our sexual encounters had been men, and two of us even had men waiting at home. Including me. I was a girlfriend to a boyfriend, a mono member of a duo. Our body parts fit together neatly.

And then there was a moment, a slippery one lubricated by hours of alcohol, where we became girl beings for whom sex was something else.

One of us kissed another, and then the pairs changed, and then we three were a triangle of bodies on a bed. And we were complete bodies, not holes to be filled.

And now we enter even more complicated calculus.

TITLE: Vamp

ART DESCRIPTION: A medieval-style painting of a unicorn.

PLACARD NOTES: A slut is a woman who sleeps with men. A dyke is a woman who sleeps with women. And the ones who do both?

We exist in a space of fetish and erasure. We are sought on dating apps as an anonymous body to spice up a heterosexual sex life. We are denied on dating apps as unreal, a phase, someone lesbians don't want to educate.

When I've fucked a heterosexual man who knows I'm bisexual, the expectations are high: I will be a sex fiend, a sex goddess, a sensual libertine, an up-for-anything being who exists for his pleasure.

When I've fucked a lesbian who knows I'm bisexual, the expectations are low: I will be working through identity stuff, and will eventually go full hetero, and my technique will be poor, and I will be a dilettante trying on queerness, able to pass, likely to phase out.

TITLE: Trollop

ART DESCRIPTION: A photograph of a full pitcher, being poured into another.

PLACARD NOTES: Beyond that, though. Bisexual and pansexual women exist in a broadened sense of sex. It isn't just P in V, or tongue in V. All encounters might be sexual; all touch may contain intent. Without clear boundaries of gender, sex is a spectrum.

And that means, in the lexicon of sex, there's more activity to be judged.

So we are super-duper sluts. Even more, we're temptresses, seductresses. We contain power for great joy and great ruin.

TITLE: Strumpet

ART DESCRIPTION: A monochrome pencil drawing of a flower covered in mud and dirt.

PLACARD NOTES: Here's a funny story: I overshot.

After having penetrative hetero sex for the first time in college, I was ruined. Dirty. My parents intimated as much, said as much, and encouraged me to move in with the guy, perhaps figuring that would get me back on the right path to marriage.

Me, at nineteen, living with a boy, playing house. And I was so close, so near to the path my teenage parents took, the path that would finally endear me to them, the path all good women must take.

He and I didn't survive college, and I thank any god who's listening for that. I dodged a bullet that would have had me speeding on to being a Mrs., a mother, an angry and bitter person like my mother and her mother.

When I didn't leave college married, and actually moved to another city, to create a life wholly unfamiliar to my family, I figured there was nothing for it but to own the title of trash, the name we all owned. And in working to own my sluttiness, I overshot. I exceeded my mother's tally by exponential numbers, my slutty grandmother's numbers by many, even my sixpence-married aunt's numbers.

So now I'm the head slut.

TITLE: Vixen

ART DESCRIPTION: A oversaturated photograph of a fox jumping, caught in midair.

PLACARD NOTES: Fucking to feel. Fucking like an animal, then fleeing into the wilderness to be free. Fucking to fight despair, depression, the desire for oblivion.

And that would all be fine. I could live with the name-calling and shame of a puritanical society. I could live with being a vixen, a tramp, a heathen, a slut.

But fucking isn't always a choice.

TITLE: Slattern

ART DESCRIPTION: Paper doll cutouts of two girl figures, connecting severed hands.

PLACARD NOTES: I'm thirteen, and Lisa and I are on the floor. Sleeping bags, blankets, pillows, all laid out by her parents. Her adopted parents, she always says. Her real mom got knocked up as a teen, gave her away. That's why she looks so different from her current parents.

She's tall. Her body is big. Her hair big. Skin darker than most. She drags one of her feet, the result of something she never talks about. Her parents, those who took her in, are small, thin, the color of street curbs. Everything in her house seems designed to accentuate her difference, to call attention to her body, moving through its space.

I'm tall too, the both of us giant thirteen-year-olds. But I look like my parents.

We lay on her blankets, looking at the room's ceiling in the dim light of the hall bulb.

He raped me, she says.

I picture him, the boy she named. Not one of our schoolmates, but someone she'd mentioned before. I filled in the lines. White, shoulder-length brown hair, slight, her height.

He raped me, she says, and tells a story that sounds like a very special episode of a TV family drama. Kindness at first, then cajoling, then threats, then force. The villain rising up after, leaving her on the floor, smiling, sneering.

She cries. I don't have words for her. My body hurts from holding it so still. My mind is already picking at the seams of the story.

I go home. Shower. Squeeze at the numb skin on my belly, arms, legs.

I live in a house that believes in the law. My dad a guardian of it. As flawed as I already see he is, how limited both my parents are in their understanding of the world, as much as I'm coming to see how law is for some people and not others, at thirteen it's my first impulse.

So I tell my parents. We are setting the table for dinner, placing forks and spoons for the five of us. I tell them the story, and they exchange glances.

She's making it up, my dad says.

Mom agrees.

Part of me knows this is false. But Lisa's story—it could have been the plot of an after-school special.

Girls cry rape for attention, my dad says.

Mom agrees.

Part of me, yeah, it knows this is wrong. But I think about how Lisa and I have been growing apart, how I've been pulling away, lured by another, prettier, more popular girl to be her homely sidekick. How there's a slight desperation to Lisa when we do hang out.

You don't want to be with a girl like that, my dad says.

Mom agrees.

It's so easy to follow instructions.

TITLE: Loose

ART DESCRIPTION: A stretched canvas depicting a woman's naked back, covered in bathroom graffiti.

PLACARD NOTES: My definition of rape has been tight and loose at once, mirroring our culture. It must be full penetration of a penis into a vagina; it must be clearly marked as assault, usually by a stranger in a dark alley; it must be accompanied by screaming and shouted nos. It must be considered negated if the girl is a slut, or dressed like a slut, or acting like a slut, or drinking like a slut; it must also be negated if the girl is a slattern, someone perceived ugly, or living on the margins, or poor trash, or disabled, or Black, or lesbian, or trans, or or or.

And by these definitions, I'm unsure of my own history.

I learned that girls make up stories about rape, that they cry for attention in the most twisted ways, that girls cannot be trusted or believed.

Which means I can't trust my own memories, dotted with big black dissociative marks as they are:

An unlit basement, a locked door, and a group of boys around me.

An unfamiliar dorm room, my shirt askew, my arms covered in sexual graffiti drawn by Sharpie, a group of human shapes circling me.

An attic, late at night, where I stop a boy, at least for a moment.

A morning before dawn, waking up to find a man having sex with me.

TITLE: Floozy

ART DESCRIPTION: A graphic vector of a box.

PLACARD NOTES: When there is a choice, and when that choice stands, I still fuck and run.

Because I have no idea how to love someone. I watched my mother and father cheat and grow to hate each other. I watched my aunt fuck her way through long lists of men and marry six of them. I watched my grandmother shut herself away after her husband died. I watched the women in my dad's family meekly obey and call it love. I watched all of them go it alone, without friends, without trust of each other.

How can you feel secure enough with someone to trust them? Lean on them? I have never known. I'm baffled when I hear stories of women who ask their partners for help, who rely on them.

Because love is rules that will be broken. Love is lying. Love is being a mirror for others. Love is control. Love is a lie, an inconvenient untruth, a doomed quest.

TITLE: Hussy

ART DESCRIPTION: A Dalí-esque portrait of melting roses and boxes of chocolate.

PLACARD NOTES: So, relationships have never lasted.

So much of a relationship revolves around subtle hints, unspoken feelings, signs and signals that have always eluded me. There are rules involved, some sort of code, for what you can and can't talk about without dissipating the mood or ruining the romance. I've never understood any of it.

I could never tell if someone was flirting until they had their tongue down my throat.

So much of a relationship can involve supposedly romantic things like spontaneity and surprises. I fear both. Routines and schedules are necessary to help me feel comfortable with social stuff, and just writing the word "surprise" makes my stomach churn.

So much of a relationship demands standard signs of love. Gifts and gestures, which confuse and scare me. Or even the simple practice of sustained eye contact; to me, it's physically painful.

So much of a relationship is chaos. It's capitulation. It's loneliness while not alone.

TITLE: Jezebel

ART DESCRIPTION: A Polaroid photograph of a woman in her underwear on a stage, mouth open in a scream.

PLACARD NOTES: In every friendship, in every romantic relationship, as far back as I can remember, I always felt a sense of playing a role. I'd argue most women feel this to an extent, balancing the schizophrenic messages our world gives us about how to behave, how to attract, how to blend in. I'd reasoned away my sense of acting as just part of being a woman.

But in my case, the acting, the masking, was never ending. Engaging with people, even those I'd gained a sense of hard-fought comfort with, was exhausting. Meeting new people was heavy. And knowing that weight, my brain would work to protect me. Run, it'd say when I faced the prospect of a new date or a new person. Flee. It's not worth the pain. No matter who gets hurt in the process.

TITLE: Tart

ART DESCRIPTION: A pointillist painting of a lone runner on an obstacle course.

PLACARD NOTES: In the relationships I did forge, I played my part so well I disappeared into it. People liked that part. I felt trapped by it.

I wanted to be loved, but more than that, I wanted to be understood. But following all the rules for relationships demanded I pretend; that prevented being truly seen and known. I could never relax, never feel comfortable.

So when I grew exhausted from playing the role and wearing the mask, panicky at the prospect of the energy needed to sustain it, I ran.

**TITLE:** Wanton

**ART DESCRIPTION:** Album cover, Liz Phair's *Exile in Guyville.*

**PLACARD NOTES:** And then in middle age I learned I was autistic. And my sluttiness took a turn.

I learned that women with autism are particularly susceptible to dangerous relationships and sexual encounters. Our confusion over social rules and practices means we miss red flags. Our need to be seen as normal means we agree to things we don't want to. Our constant masking means we are convinced and coerced more easily; we betray ourselves in order to be liked.

Add to that the wariness I learned as part of the women in my family . . .

Add to that the grotesque and contradictory nature of the rules for women in this world . . .

Add to that everything, everywhere, everyone, every each all infinity . . .

I'm so tired, so fucking tired.

So I've set aside relationships, and even sex, as the only way to be safe.

**TITLE:** Quean

**ART DESCRIPTION:** An Instagram reel with a white background on which emoji stickers click past with *Yass Qween* and *100% That Bitch.*

**PLACARD NOTES:** An old word, an archaic word, yet one that seems so apt. It echoes back to us, as the word for an overly forward, impudent, or even just a "robust" young woman.

It's too forward to share all of this about sex and sluts; it's impudent to think about and speak about internalized rape culture; it's too much to analyze modern romance and behaviors from a disability point of view.

And yet it's also cause for celebration, cause for affirmations on social media, cause for funny memes and sarcastic posts and more, so much more, so many more words and thoughts and states of being in the span of microseconds.

It's too much and it's not enough.

TITLE: Spinster

ART DESCRIPTION: A package of the Old Maid card game.

PLACARD NOTES: I've aged. I'm deep in my forties. A slut, but on sabbatical. I have reached peak spinster.

In the past, that term applied to white women who were not picked, who were passed over in the marriage lottery, who were never penetrated by a man. If she was of the gentry, she lived with her parents, a financial burden no man would take on. And maybe she'd write some books, like the Brontë sisters, or maybe she'd just fade away into nothingness, like all the unnamed women of yore. If she was working class, she'd work, and perhaps live in servants' quarters in a gentry home, and dodge rape by the master, and one day become the head of the house, the stern figure in many a gothic novel.

I live in a house, one I paid for myself, and I live alone, a configuration I chose myself. I don't currently date, and don't have plans to. I have reached the age where a woman fades into invisibility, no longer young and fuckable. A used-up, busted-up fuck doll who's ready for the trash.

By taking a break from being a slut, I protect myself from sensory overload, from the invasion of my personal space, from the social requirements of being around another person, from the confusing rules of romance, from the ache of wearing a mask for too long.

I want to unlearn the rules of sex. I want to unlearn the givens, the ways men are the actors, the ways women are the acted upon; the rules of predator and prey. I want to unlearn the terms, redefine sexuality and being. I want to unlearn pain, and trauma, and the lessons that came from them. I want to unlearn the ideas of disability, and what counts as normal and valued. I want to unlearn it all.

TITLE: Bitch

ART DESCRIPTION: A copy of the seminal feminist magazine *Bitch*.

PLACARD NOTES: Because I've had sex to please someone. And I've had sex because it was easier than saying no. I've had sex to prove something to a partner; I've had sex to prove something to myself. I've had sex because I was unconscious. I've had sex to see myself in someone else's eyes. I've had sex because I was in love; I've had sex because I was falling out of love. I've had sex to be considered cool. I've had sex because I found a person unbearably hot. I've had sex because I was incredibly turned on. I've had sex because I was fantasizing about someone I shouldn't. I've had sex because masturbation wasn't enough. I've had sex because I knew I would at least get to masturbate later. I've had sex because I wanted to. I've had sex because I thought I should. I've had sex because it was expected. I've had sex to discover a new identity. I've had sex because sometimes, occasionally, it is a transcendent experience. I've had sex because I wanted to engage with life. I've had sex because I was depressed and wanted to feel something else. I've had sex because I wanted to feel normal. I've had sex because I wasn't comfortable with neurotypical communication and rules, but I could understand sex.

I've had sex for the reasons my mom did, and my aunt, and my grandma. I've had sex to connect, communicate. I've had sex in ways that show how truly similar we are; how different from the women in my family I'm not.

I've had sex for all of these reasons and none; I've had sex for reasons of others' and of my own.

And I will have sex again, even though I'm aging, even though I'm on a break. I will have sex that's meh, and I will have sex that's excellent, and I will have sex that builds on a deep connection, and I will have sex that is only for a moment. I will have sex. And hopefully, it will be unlearned, newly defined.

I'm a slut, I'm a slattern, I'm a spinster. I'm a bitch, and a dyke, and a vixen. I'm bisexual and autistic and exhausted.

So here I am, and how dare I speak about that? How dare I take a modicum of pleasure in these words, old and new, words I should be ashamed to hear? How dare I?

# Abjection and Other A Words

*Avondale*. On a frigid December night in 2012, shortly before I decide to leave Chicago, I walk under the overpass at Belmont and Kedzie. The cars race above, their sounds magnified against steel and emptiness. Loud, cold, dark. A place to rush through. But there are mattresses, ad hoc beds, wedged between the massive concrete columns holding up the Kennedy. Piles of blankets and rags on each, covering bodies, alive and nearly not. Time seems slower here, space thicker. I want to speed up, push past this abject scene. But there's a pull, a different level of gravity slowing me down. They want me to see their world. They want to remind me what lies underneath.

*Addison*. It's the street where the Chicago Cubs live. The street that people in other cities and states know. In the summer of 2000, when I move to Chicago after graduating college, I know nothing of the city, or anyone living there. In my last semester of college, I blocked off Sunday afternoons to visit the computer lab and send off résumés to jobs in Boston, DC, San Francisco. Anywhere, everywhere. Take me, I pleaded with each email. Give me a reason to leave Iowa. A company in Chicago did. Addison is the magic word I use to explain myself, to justify this incomprehensible act of leaving. No one leaves. No one does things different than what came before. But I have, and I tell people back home who love sports above all else: my apartment is three blocks from Addison. I say: I live near Wrigley Field. I agree: the Cubs are looking good this year.

*Anecdote*. The day I move into my studio apartment, unpacking my meager boxes of college mementoes and hand-me-down dishes, the radio is on. A local station plays "Sweet Home Chicago," the Blues Brothers' version. I'm an atheist, and agnostic of signs, but this feels like one. I will relate this story whenever anyone asks what I love about Chicago, deeply misunderstanding the question.

*A grid*. For two weeks in June, before my job starts, I walk the city. I teach myself the grid, using a fold-up neighborhood map. I ride buses and trains, memorizing stops and block counts. I discover there are no public bathrooms in the Loop, and I pay twice the amount for snacks and water and beer. But there's romance to these days. They are numbered, and they are infinite, and they are mine alone. This, this city, this will be mine. This will be where I am seen.

*Avondale*. For the thirteen years I lived in Chicago, I treated the city like I do any romance—handing myself over fully, becoming a disciple, losing my head full of grids and plans and hope in the process.

*Acquirement*. When all you want to do is read and write, there is no place for you in capitalism. The company that invited me to Chicago knows this. Leo Burnett's media agency, Starcom, recruits college seniors like me, big groups of us across the Midwest, with vague job descriptions emphasizing creativity. They hook kids like me, with no experience of wealth, by showcasing long lists of perks reflecting the largesse of the time: client meetings at Wrigley Field, client meetings at spas, client meetings at restaurants with astronomically priced food, client meetings in bedrooms after unlimited bar tabs. I am in uncharted territory—the only one from back home to graduate college, the only one to leave, the only one to have a job of the mind. So I fall easily.

*Amy*. I meet another Amy at work, a newly minted graduate like me. She's the first to say it out loud: maybe we're trapped in this place of Excel sheets and PowerPoint decks and endless emails, shilling for pharmaceuticals and big beef. Maybe we made a mistake. And now we can't leave, not without paying the company back for some of the "free" perks. And we can't make our rent, despite getting free manicures and free dinners and free booze and free things we never asked for. She is the first to give language to the feeling of terror that at age twenty-three, leaving home to find something better, working so hard to do things differently than my baby-faced parents who worked and worked just to age, I have ended up in the same place.

*Alcohol.* I discovered the magic in college. Drunk, I learned I can shut down my brain, which is always seeking out danger and looking for lessons in how to be human. I can be normal with alcohol. So in Chicago, it's my tool, my medication, my life jacket. Everyone drinks, all the time. Being social is drinking. So suddenly, I make friends easily. Or, said another way, others choose me more quickly, more easily.

*August.* I meet him as summer wanes in 2000, at an apartment party on Addison, filled with fraternity brothers who formed a tech company. We smoke out on the porch, and we make out in the drunk early morning hours, and I stay with him for ten years before fleeing on another early morning.

*Avondale.* I hopped apartments after leaving him, finally landing here. The place I can afford, the place on the outer reaches of the city I'd known with him, full of white people and white jobs and white wealth. Here, this neighborhood, reminds me of home—auto shops and harried moms on buses and liquor stores and people with color in their skin. It should soothe me in a way, help me transition from one era to another. But I'm breaking down.

*Amy.* I meet another Amy through a friend of a friend. She lives in that apartment building on Addison, so close to Wrigley you can hear the crowds cheer and jeer. The landlord makes the tenants move their cars for every home game so he can charge thirty bucks for tourist parking.

*A scene.* The first time he shows himself, shows the push and pull he will exert on me, is a few weeks after that August party. He makes a scene because I won't leave the Addison apartment and come with him, won't set aside my friends for him. I'm embarrassed, and confused, and turn to my new friends for understanding. We, three twenty-three-year-old girls, are young and clueless. We mistake his intensity, his animal eyes, for ardor and for adulthood. For being special and loved. We laugh, and drink more, and see nothing beyond the night.

*Abundance.* The city has everything, and he and his fraternity friends have the money to buy it. We go to clubs, and the boys pay for bottle service and beautiful girls with black cards, and we go to massive condos purchased with dot-com sales, and we ride boats financed by cocaine sales, and we go to Miami and Las Vegas and California. He had school paid for, and has no debt, and makes four times my salary. They all do.

*A memory.* Growing up on the east side of Des Moines, I thought Red Lobster was unbearably fancy, and too expensive for the family.

*Adulation.* He says I am a dream girl. He says I am gorgeous. He says he can't stand to be apart from me. He says he needs me. It doesn't really matter who he is, or what I think of him. He is a man, twenty-six, surrounded by friends, supported by family. I am swept up by all the talking, all the things he says, all the rules I can internalize.

*A change.* I leave the job that brought me to the city, find another promising creativity, find it disappoints as well. But it's at Northwestern University, a prestigious name that plays well with his friends, a name that confuses the family back home enough to say nothing. The job pays more, and it gives me another perk: part-time grad school tuition at 85 percent off the ticket price.

*Academics.* Because the city isn't enough anymore to prove my worth. I take on Chicago as an identity. Living there makes me special, makes me different than everyone back home. Makes me worthwhile. But that's fading already, a year in. So I return to my proven method of validation—school. I get a master's degree. Years later I'll get another one. I'm seeking out something, anything, to help me make sense of this world. Help show me my place in it.

*Attachment.* I said it doesn't matter who he is. And that's true, but also false. He is from a small town. A white straight boy from a town of white straight boys. He is paid for, college fully funded, by generational wealth. He is known and appreciated, the son of the main wealthy family in his town. He is creative, or has enough original ideas about art and photography for a young man to be named creative, to be encouraged and loved. That's all it takes for a twentysomething boy to be interesting to a twentysomething girl in Chicago in the year 2000. That's all it takes for a boy to feel like he has earned love, to believe he can and should control who he chooses to love.

*Adjoined.* Two years in, we pool our stuff and get an address to share. It's an old temple, an apartment I can't afford. Thirty-foot ceilings, stained glass, a balcony looking out over ivy. We live on a street named for an English palace, and it feels regal, the richest thing. Turn left from our door and we go to Boystown, calling me with whispers of the future. Turn right and we hit Broadway with bookstores and diners and bagels. We host parties. We drink and smoke all night. We listen to music and watch stolen videos. We live. I'm happy. We're happy. This is happiness. This is happiness? This is . . .

*Arithmetic.* I try to pull my weight. I don't like feeling bought. But I also don't like our fights. I tell him, after yet another dinner with his friends, where I try to order frugally, where two rich boys buy the most expensive bottles of wine, where the boys insist yet again on splitting the cost among us all, and I don't have the money, so on the credit card it goes, like all the other times, like groceries and rent and everything to keep pace; I tell him how frustrated I am. It's just money, he says, mouth curled in disgust. You need to budget better.

*Aftermath.* It never adds up. The math never breaks in my favor.

*Author.* It's my secret dream, one I share with him. I want to write books, like those that kept me alive as a kid. So I do it, I write during the temple years, and it's shit because I haven't written enough, haven't lived enough. There will be plenty of living in the next years, plenty of eyes opening, plenty of growing. But now, in the mid-2000s, I fail, again and again. So I give up on writing for years, recede into a life of working and partying and getting smaller every day.

*An exodus.* The thing about big cities: there's a time limit. You move to the city at age twenty-three, and you party, and you build a résumé, and you have sex, and you think you're original, the only people who've ever done what you're doing. And when you've been doing that for a few years, everyone pairs off. And you go to your first wedding, and then your second, and then your thirtieth. And if you're smart you sneak in your own wedding somewhere early on, so you get to be original in your place settings and your bagpipes and your horse-drawn carriages and your landmark location. And you stay in the city for a bit, until you get pregnant, and then the suburbs call, and most of you are from the suburbs anyway, your parents warm and welcoming and wealthy and wanting to help with grandkids. And everyone is doing it, a mass exodus of white people in their late twenties, doing what they're supposed to do. Then suddenly the only people left in the city are the ones who do a lot of drugs and the guys still hoping for a model to love them for their money and that couple with the girl who won't marry or have kids, the one no one wants to talk to anymore because they make you wonder things about your own motivations, make you wonder if you really like mowing your suburban lawn or staying home with the sudden brood of kids. And the ones left behind, me and him, it's time for our reckoning.

*Avondale.* I'm drinking constantly. Heavily. I'm drinking to oblivion and beyond. I'm drinking alone. I call it freedom, this ability to drink without his judgment. I call it calm, the way my muscles quit on me. But the end of the night, when I have to stop drinking and go to bed, is the most terrifying, terrible time. Because real life awaits again in the morning.

*Advertising.* It becomes my career, without really choosing it. I write words to sell things, first at the university, then freelance, and then at agencies, and I start making decent money at it, and I occasionally remember the anarchist dreams I had with Amy. But by now she's married with a couple kids, running a mom blog.

*A condo.* He and I, we leave our temple, perhaps pushed by all our friends buying property and being adults, or perhaps because even the thirty-foot ceilings aren't tall enough to hold all his anger and my things unsaid. We buy a condo in Ukrainian Village in 2008, before the crash. We can't afford it, and that means I especially can't afford it, but we do it, and this will be happiness, this will be next.

*A fragment.* The two years we spend in the condo are partly shadowed, pushed out of conscious memory. Clear, though, is the gray office carpet, where I often sink down, curling my body around itself, waiting for him to stop. The hallways, where our sweet cat turns somersaults, asking for love while her humans lose it. The walk-in closet, where I return in tears to change my clothes after he says I look fat or slutty or inappropriate. The sound of the door when he comes home, my quick breaths while I arrange my face and body to be pleasing. The bitter winter air that leaks through the poorly insulated patio door, no matter how much weather tape I layer; forevermore, the bite of a poorly insulated windows will bring me to panicky, blind tears.

*Affirmation.* He says I'm ugly without the right clothes, the right makeup, the right hair. He says I am too fat, and he says I am difficult when I diet. He says he will record me, make me listen to myself, hear the hard facts of my pathetic self. He says he has crushes on people at work, younger girls, hotter girls. He says I am broken. He says I am crazy. He says I am pitiful, the way I curl into a ball against the wall when he starts in on me, the way I retreat into myself, the way I let him spew hatred at me. I am swept up again by all the talking, all the things he says, all the rules I continue to internalize.

*A child.* He wants one. We've been unmarried and childless for nearly a decade. I've changed everything else to please him. But this is the principle that I need to cling to. His friends have left the city, and he's lonely and lost. They are all married with kids, and from his view, they have achieved meaning, as if it is a high score at an arcade. They have made their lives worthwhile. And look at us, look at you—is this it? It can't be. A kid. A kid will help.

*Awareness.* I know a kid will not help. I know this. I know this act of procreation will not grant meaning and worth; I know it will only bring a child into a family who hurts and calls it love. I know this, remember it, in those black spots of my childhood that I block. I know these facts, and cling to them, but that knowledge, that awareness, begins to fray and crack as he talks and taunts and twists. As he flays the bits of skin he hasn't yet touched. Who will you be otherwise, he asks? What will you do as we get older? How will you matter?

*Adage.* He says, We aren't fighting. We don't fight. We are the couple everyone wants to be. You're pathetic. You don't make sense. You don't know what's best for you. This is for your own good. You're an embarrassment. You embarrass me. Don't make me do this.

*Autism.* And when he says these things and many others, I go mute. I shut down. It enrages him when I do this. I don't know that mutism and shutdowns are a behavior many autistic people experience, especially when combined with traumatic situations. All I know is no matter what I say it is picked apart, twisted around, turned back as a sharper weapon. It is proof I am everything he says. So I say nothing.

*Ass.* He wants it. The asshole, specifically. He wants to fuck my ass. I don't want him to fuck my ass. We can't break up over anal sex, he says. We can't end here, he says. So? he asks, waiting for me to give in.

*Ashamed.* My ass is a source of pain. Every day, for years and years, I smile at bosses and colleagues, at parents, at him, and push my anger and stress back into my body. Often, sometimes weekly, sometimes daily, that rage and repression make my intestines seize and cramp, my knees buckle, sweat pops across my cheeks and down my back. The pressure and pain make me vomit, or cry, or both. After hours of this, my ass finally spews liquid shit and stink, tearing and burning, as I pant in relief. So I am ashamed of my ass. It is a mortifying thing to leave a bar early for fear of shitting my pants, to cry and plead with the person in line for the port-a-potty at Lollapalooza to let me in, to panic and shake in rooms without obvious bathrooms and exits. My ass is embarrassing, unpredictable, raw.



*Angry*. But he wants it. He wants to fuck my painful, shameful ass. Bored of the other holes, maybe. Pissed at me, for not changing my mind on kids and marriage as he has. Enraged, denied something, when usually, mostly, I give in to his demands, desperate to avoid another fight.

*Animal*. A few times, early in our relationship, fucking me from behind, he tried pushing himself into my ass. When I gently pulled away and guided him back to the hole I was offering, he never said a word. I didn't either. Even then, I was ceding myself by staying silent. Ten years later, he reads me articles by women describing the incredible orgasms they have from being fucked in the ass. He says I am crazy to pass it up. He says I am being selfish. He says he will have to cheat if I deny him.

*Abuse*. Years later, I still don't feel confident calling my partner's actions abuse. I fear I'm diluting the word. Back then he manipulated, punished, controlled, but with words instead of fists. He never pushed me down to the floor, but I ended up there, and he liked the view.

*Asshole*. What is the demarcation between being an asshole and being an abuser? Is it a bruise where no one can see it? Hidden under clothes but visible on the naked skin? Do bruises inside count, swelling in the parts of the brain that contain the shape of you, the home of neurons that fire and create confidence, worth, and dignity? Does a battered brain, swollen vessels and flesh choking off the memories of yourself, matter? Shame exists in shadow, in the deep purple of inflamed tissue, in the blistered and pus-filled crevices of our bodies. In wounds tangible and invisible. In the belief love is control, dissatisfaction, blame.

*Admission.* Remember: women are liars. I learned that again and again growing up. We exaggerate, we hyperbolize. We make things up for attention. We claim abuse just to tear a man down. I don't want to be that kind of girl, the one who can't take a joke, who's too sensitive, who can't get into a discussion without tearing up and calling it a fight. Even though I don't have the language yet, I know there is a shameful part of me, a part that has to play a role to get through social situations, has to wear a mask to appear normal. That part of me depends on others to tell me what normal is; that part has to playact at being human. I am a deception. A liar indeed. So I deserve punishment.

*Abjection.* He wants my ass. He's claimed every other part of me. Demands I lose weight, dress nice, paint my face, fix my hair that is falling out in clumps. Commands I say what he wants, and apologize every time I get it wrong. But he wants more. I try to calm my stomach and my ass. I go to doctors and get medicines, I try charting my food and weight and activity. But my bad stomach persists and will for our ten years. It will get worse in the last two years. My body is screaming. Look in your bed, it says. The rot starts there.

*Audit.* Just as my body screams for my attention by making my ass a disaster zone, his mind fixates on my ass as the source of our problems. He wants to control the uncontrollable. And when I finally apologize for everything I do and don't do, and it isn't enough for him, when our final fight stretches over days, days where I shriek inside a mute shell, I start to see.

*An early February morning.* I flee. My ass, the contested territory, the canary in the coal mine, calms when I leave.

*Approval.* For weeks and months after, I make lists. Reasons I left. I read and reread the lists. He calls, emails, texts. Demanding an explanation for leaving so suddenly, without any provocation. Demanding time so he can explain how my antidepressants have made me psycho. Demanding I see reason. I come back to those lists again and again, trying to dislodge his voice in my head. All the things I was wrong about. All the ways I disappointed him. All the reasons I should give in, return to him.

*Avondale*. Two years I live in the city after leaving him, and it's still rotten with him. I run everywhere in the city, running running running, running in clothes designed for running, sloughing off bits of myself to be smaller, running from apartment to apartment looking for a home, running from job to job to find something, anything, to give me worth, running from bed to bed to feel something, feel a bit of warming or scorching flame.

*Age*. The thing about cities: there's an age limit. You move there in your twenties, pioneers and explorers, claiming the land for you and your brethren. But you have to do your work quick, and move on. You must leave the city by your thirties, or you'll see the new wave moving in, the conquering youth, remaking the city in their image. If you see this, see the usurpers, you see your own mortality. You notice the hangovers are worse, and the clothes in style are weird and ill-fitting, and the L commute is a terrible slog of heat or cold that sucks hours from your day, hours in which you notice everyone on the train is younger than you. You notice eyes skimming over you, when before your youth would make them snag. You also see the pattern, that you were once the assholes without hangovers, that you gave those older than you visions of their own impermanence. Once you see this, you can't unsee. You start spotting the wizened woman on the train and the hangdog man on the bus, the only ones older than you, and you see what the city does to those who don't leave.

*Attrition*. I saw it before, how white my neighborhoods and offices and commutes are. I read the histories of the city, how the Daley empire policies and projects and public works meant segregation now and forever. I knew which areas to avoid, which streets to lock your car doors, which L routes to skip, the reasoning always unstated but understood. I saw how the city was deliberately divided and how we as youth, each generation, kept it going. But I saw it without seeing it. When my life broke, and I couldn't afford the past, and I gave away all my belongings, to flee, to be rid of him, I started to see different parts of the city. Different routes, different people. I saw myself, my ignorant interloping. And all the lore, all the mystique, the specialness, the reasons I chose Chicago . . . there was nothing left. The city was a place that hurts and hurts and hurts, grinding up bodies who are not white or young or able.

*Avondale*. That overpass, those mattresses, the barely alive bodies. Underneath the gilded city. I see more and more every day in my last year, the ragged men and women crowding the Loop's streets with signs pleading for help, the barefoot woman sobbing in an alley next to a Chipotle, the bodies who sleep in the pedestrian walkway under Macy's. Chicago is not magic, and it does not make anyone better.

*Abscond*. I fled Des Moines in 1995 to go to college, be different from my family, be special. I fled Iowa in 2000 to be made over, to chart new ground, to be the one who created something new. I fled him in 2011. And finally, in 2013, I flee Chicago. I move back to Des Moines, for reasons I try to make pretty and practical: it is cheaper, and it is cooler from a development renaissance over a decade, and it is connected, the place of family. Really, I have nowhere else to go.

*An anecdote*. That's what Chicago is now. I used to live in Chicago, I say. If I'm asked why, I chalk it up to youth, to the lack of creative jobs in Iowa in 2000, to the kind of terrified bravery I still possess. If I'm asked why I left, I say the city changed, that I changed. I lie, to them and myself.

*Address*. I have a house now. I had a few apartments at first. But the year I turned forty, I wanted a home with rooms and stairs, something unimaginable in Chicago. I bought an old house, built in 1910, with multiple floors and big windows and a wraparound porch and trees, so many trees. I mow the yard, and I rake leaves, and talk with friends about plants and heating maintenance. I live alone, and I can breathe. And my nightmares, the ones where I'm frozen in a crouch, wedged against a wall, coerced and convinced to go back, they don't visit as much anymore.

*Abuse.* When you don't know what love is supposed to be, how do you know if it's abuse? When you don't know your brain is different, how do you trust it? In the years after I left, I told myself that he had changed. That he was sweet and smart and kind when we met, and we had our rough patches, but only toward the end did he turn vicious. But nearly ten years after our breakup, I reread my journals from our time together. And I saw things I had buried. Right from the start, he had to push, to pick, to start fights that confused and intimidated me. Because he was weak. And I didn't see it. I only saw the way out of a fight, picking a path through rocks and overgrown bush and broken beer bottles toward safety. Apologizing along the way, always, for everything, for nothing. I didn't have language then, not for relationships. I didn't understand grooming. I didn't see how all the early doting and loving and attention could be dangerous, how he would transform when I didn't respond the way he wanted to the doting and loving and attention. How he punished me. Again, not with fists or weapons. But it hurt, and I couldn't figure out why. I couldn't figure out why it didn't feel right, but it looked right to everyone else.

*Afterimage.* Do you see it? I didn't. In the years after, I fucked and ran, so desperately confused about what happened with him. I saw him in everyone. Nowhere, no one was safe. All these years later, I still feel that fear. I feel the need to write more, to lay it all out, to draw charts and graphs, an X + Y axis that demonstrates that I'm not lying, that I'm not seeking attention, that I'm not unjustified. I want to give you proof, even as I chip away at the language I use. I want you to believe me. Please believe me.

*A family.* So here I am, returned to the city of origin. My family is here, and they showed themselves, so they have faded out of my life. I found something else here, though. I knew Eric in college, and when I moved back, I emailed him on a whim. He welcomed me, introduced me to his friends.

We're all fortysomething now, most of us childless, most of us gay in some way. And I have met more friends, writers and creatives and podcasters. I have found a family.

*Author*. I started to write again, and kept going, and got better and better, and I have turned my years of living into art.

*Avondale*. I had an address there. I had a vision there. I left there, and have started again.

# Dead Souls

I often write fictional stories. And some of them are based on things that happened. This is what writers do. We use what we see, what we experience, to tell other stories.

But sometimes, we use fiction to work things out. We dance around the truth and memory, and call it a story, a figment. Because claiming it as real, as nonfiction, is dangerous.

This is a story that took me years to write. It is fiction. But it's also nonfiction. It can be both.

—

I knew the sounds a body made. When my hands pushed and kneaded a trapezius, or a quadricep, or a gluteus, and that movement crossed the line between pain and pleasure, back and forth, when the body yielded, or when the frame resisted, there were gradients of sighs, degrees of breathing. A code that the best of us learned, and responded to with a bit more pressure, or a bit less precision.[1]

Because I knew these things, because I made money with my knowledge of bodies, most men expected magic when we had sex for the first time. Masseuses were a rarity when I started in 1979, and for much of the next decade.[2]

1 What's true and what's not? Here's something that creates a difference: I was never a massage therapist.

2 Another untruth. This was not the year.

Spas belonged to the warm deserts of Ojai and Phoenix, not this cold tundra of Minneapolis.[3]

When I explained my job, men imagined fingers that could work spells, muscles that could squeeze in all places they wanted. The polite and the pushy assumed I was a slut. I was the kind of girl who put out without a ring, a women's libber, a punk, a freak. So they were lazy in bed, watching and waiting for me to do my work.[4]

Maybe that's why Graham was different.[5] He knew what I needed, knew I wanted someone else to do the work for once.

"Let me move you," he said our first time. We'd met at a bar, and went home to his apartment, and played Joy Division.[6] He laid me on my back, rubbed his thin soft fingers over my skin and breasts, rolled his black-haired knuckles over my tongue and lips. Eased my legs and hips into place. In his bed, which became our bed, my body found my own sounds.

—

You, though. You were different too. Your ash blond hair, long on your head, curled at the ends, thick across your chest. Your tongue that curled over and around English words and accented the wrong syllables. Your name, which sounded like a whisper, a breath. A command. *Ilias*.[7]

—

3 See how much I'm changing things? Working to separate the reality from this fiction? Trying to create clear lines, so no one can read this and find me out? I'm hiding. That's what fiction can do too.

4 I'm creating a fiction imbued with reality. I wasn't a massage therapist, but these are the kinds of things people expect when they hear I'm bisexual: an oversexed slut who needs no recognition as human.

5 A different name, of course. All the names are different. And even more so—I've changed all the names in this book. Tried to give everyone privacy and protect myself. But here—I felt I had to go even further and change names again.

6 Even the little details I'm changing. Where we met, what we listened to. By moving these events to a different fictional year, it helps me make these changes. Helps me obfuscate.

7 I'm hiding him too. Changing all his details so he can be protected. That's what I tell myself.

With each breath on my table I heard release, at least for a little while, from money disappearing into college funds and debt, cutthroat competition for work titles, dying parents in spare bedrooms, spouses sleeping on couches. When I told them *let me move you*, told them not to resist, told them to fight their instincts and let me do my work, they did. Even the men, trained to hear women's commands as vapor, their resistance as banter.[8]

It was satisfying, seeing and hearing what my hands did. That's what I told Graham in those first months, and years, when he presented me with pride to his friends and parents. I was his witchy girlfriend who could touch you and heal you for money. I was both the harbinger of the future and a throwback to ancient times.

He turned deposits into pensions and retirement funds.[9] I turned knots of muscle into supple tissue and release. "We're marking the world, you know." In this way, he said, we'd be known. We wouldn't disappear upon death.

I loved Graham for the image he had of us, the one he gave me.[10]

---

You, though. You understood intimately what we did.

You joined the spa on my fifth anniversary with Graham. You were a genuine Swede, the owner said proudly, as if that fact would give us, this place, legitimacy.

A few weeks in, you told me about the open sore you found on a man's foot. I told you about the dead toe belonging to a trust-fund kid.

You said something, then, in your first language, harsh consonants and soft sighs, that translated loosely to money lacking beauty.

Months of this, our schedules syncing and our ease with each other growing. I started cataloging each body, looking for the stories I could tell you

8 To write this, I imagined myself as a masseuse. I imagined myself in this year. I used the experiences of now and then, transplanted them. That's what fiction writers do, especially when they're trying to tell a story in code. But a side effect—this can be a very depressing exercise. I understand how little our world has changed.

9 He did something equally boring.

10 That image—that's what sustained me, kept me going, even during the years when I sank to the floor and stayed there.

later. That look on your face as I'd describe the farting matron or the acne-covered back. Your thick eyebrows raising, your lips carving a smile in your blond beard, your pale cheeks sprouting red flashes. I held my breath waiting for that smile.[11]

—

"Loving someone means we matter," Graham said once, as we ate greasy steak tacos after a night of drinking. The grease absorbed the vodka. His words mingled with the sour cream, tasting salty and sweet at once.

He ate fast, almost angry. Crunching and huffing. Resenting the need for food, like he resented the need for sleep. He could do so much more with that time, he said. He could finally create the photographs he always talked about, write the book he always talked about. "I could be everything I wanted without sleep," he said, laughing, his grin nearing a grimace. I loved that. I loved that he picked me. I loved that someone with dreams and drive loved me.[12]

One night, playing pool at a dive bar, we learned his high school best friend and his wife were pregnant. After the announcement, I'd gone to the bathroom and changed my soaked tampon. In the toilet bowl my blood seeped into the water, creating ribbons of red. I watched it with relief.

We didn't need kids, Graham said at the taco stand. "We'll be each other's family," he said. Then he slipped a ring on my finger.[13]

—

You and I, we released people from the rigor of their bodies. You said it was like letting a soul run free, even if only for a little while. The last I'd thought

11 We worked together somewhere else. The closeness though, that was real.

12 We had creative dreams, and that's another thing that kept me going. Someone who seemed to prize the things I did, who wanted to make a mark. He gave up on that long before he said he did. Long before I did.

13 In reality, we never married. I never wanted it, and amazingly, I held on to that through all the bad years, when he came to think marriage and kids would replace art, would be the way to make his mark. And just like everyone who thinks that, he thought he was totally original in the idea.

of souls was back in church as a child. I'd long put those teachings aside. But when you talked about souls, I wanted to believe. Maybe souls had their mates. Maybe that explained this connection we had, growing, taking up more space, filling in the gaps Graham had left behind.[14]

—

In Graham's twenties, it was sexy to fuck a woman as much as he wanted without any fear of being trapped, a woman who would have an abortion without even bothering him for the co-pay. In his midthirties, he helped rich white men retire, and they paid him more money and gave him new titles. But he hadn't created the photos he wanted, or the book. He hadn't done the things that he thought would make him known. After our courthouse wedding, that look became more guarded. Suspicious. His black eyebrows, spotted with gray, a bit more unruly than the hair on his head, the hair that was receding, curled inward instead of up. Disapproval instead of delight.

"My dad's life is so small," he said, over more greasy steak tacos after another night of drinking. "If he didn't have me, who'd remember him after he dies?" I thought about our friends, the ones who had married in elaborate Catholic weddings with open bars, the ones who moved out to three-story new-construction homes in the suburbs, who had little boys and girls who looked like them.

I reminded Graham of our refrains. Love made us eternal, love made us family, love made us live after death. I told him we would find life's purpose together. The lyrics were becoming worn with use, like the surf songs of our high school times now playing on radio stations as "classics."[15]

He ate, chomping at his steak and lettuce as he did, fast and angry. "I wonder if our daughter would look like you," he said.

At home, I hugged him. He felt smaller. I was afraid to squeeze him, or lean on him. I was afraid to breathe. We were in the 1980s, and politicians were battling for the nation's souls.[16] Battling against women like me, women

14 Do you see what's happening? Do you know what this story is about?

15 Grunge.

16 We were twenty years later, and politicians were battling with even more fervor and lunacy, with more still to come.

who would not allow their bodies to be bred. Dead inside, us women. Refusing men their natural birthright.

At some point, Graham stopped hugging me.

—

But you hugged me, and I felt supported again.

Then we went home, exhausted, grimy, full of the breath of other people. We went home, me to my husband and you to your wife.

That night Graham invited you, all our coworkers, to a party at our apartment. You and I found ourselves out on my patio smoking a cigarette, and we watched cars below us, a stream heading west, toward the suburbs, where your parents watched your six-month-old baby. You and I watched the cars and the city lights and sat still and silent and alone and breathed each other's air, and we thought about bodies and breath, souls, lives lived differently, and I felt content for a moment, a moment I lived in for the coming weeks.[17]

—

I trained myself to stay still in the bed Graham and I shared. He said I twitched, kicked, even slapped. He laughed in the mornings, chronicling his bruises.

"Your body knows something you don't," he said.

So I slept carefully, woke often to ensure my position on my side of the queen bed. I laid next to the cold brick wall that faced west, pushed against it.[18] I woke in the morning with my teeth clenched shut, my neck rigid, my legs aching and bloodless.

He pointed more and more to the suburban friends, to their children who would carry their names and genes and memories forward. He pointed to them and said they had meaning in their lives. What did we have?

I thought of those friends, how many gin and tonics they had when they snuck away to the city for the night, how much they sniped at each other across barstools and poker tables on those nights, how their bodies deflated when it was time to go home.

17 Sometimes I still do.

18 Sometimes, so many years later, I still have nightmares about being back in that bed, against that wall.

I pushed back on Graham, at first. I reminded him of all the things we'd said. I made jokes about how miserable life's meaning must make people.

But his breath turned into panting, as he worked himself into a rage that would span days.

I shut down and shut up, curled my hands around my knees, looked down at the floor, knowing anything I said would be classified as wrong. Finally I'd apologize, for anything and everything, for nothing.

I shrank in size, kept myself in check. My body rigid, my soul stuck.[19]

I hated the people on my massage table then. I hated the sounds they made, so animal and raw. I hated the smells, sweat and dirt and decay. I hated that I had to touch them, and by touching them, by releasing all the fury and frustration of their small and hollow lives, I was infected by them. I absorbed what they let go.

---

That's how I explained you. You understood that hatred. But more than that: you liked me large and unstuck and raw. I could take up space with you. I could remember the shape of me.

You were stuck too. That's what I told myself. Your wife had changed, your life had changed, and what you'd believed to be true had shifted and morphed under your feet.[20]

We laughed, you and me. There was no censoring ourselves. No rage to dodge, no tears to duck. We laughed in the empty, austere common room, over packed lunches of chicken and rice or bologna sandwiches. We laughed at the staff meetings, laughed over coffee under halogen light.

We laughed at the kinesiology convention in November, the one in San Antonio, the one that was two days of workshops and product fairs, and one night free. You wanted to sit outside on the River Walk that night, in the dry breeze, so different from the Minnesota wind that was already brittle back home. You ordered a whiskey and a burger, and I didn't want to make any

19 You already read a version of this called an "essay," denoting its truth. Here I've turned it only slightly, changed the merest of details, and called it fiction. Lying, just like a woman.

20 The things we tell ourselves are fiction merged with nonfiction.

decisions, so I followed your lead. When you ordered more whiskey, I did too.[21]

You suggested we walk, and we left the River Walk and cut down side streets, looking in house windows for warm-weather layouts and real Texans, tracing lines of graffiti on shop walls.

Outside the hotel, I brushed aside cigarette butts with my foot and sat on the sidewalk and lit my own. You took a picture of me with your Polaroid. When you shook it out and showed it to me, I saw someone else. I wanted to step into that picture, slip into that woman's easy smile, shrug on the freedom in her limbs. That woman would do what she wanted.[22]

Inside, you hugged me again. I smelled my cigarette in your hair, and felt the whiskey in your cheek. My arms shook a little as they curled around your neck.

I leaned on you, and you leaned back.

We turned our heads, and you kissed me, or I kissed you, and we were kissing. Then we were running. My boots and your sneakers pounding the stairs to the second floor, laughing, shaking, hiccupping, holding sweaty hands. I didn't think of Graham, and you didn't think of your wife, and we ran faster, down the second floor, to your room, so that would be true.

You turned the hall light on. You backed me up against the wall. You put your hands under my shirt, and then lifted it off. You kissed me, and peeled me, piece by piece.

There was no music. No need to set a mood.

I surprised you then. Surprised myself too. I pushed you, toward the bed. I peeled you layer by layer, then looked at you.

You spoke. *Finally.*

21 Some of this happened, in a different city, a different time. But some of this is fiction. Some is what I wanted to happen, and what he wanted to happen, a thing we would imagine together later once feelings were admitted. A missed opportunity, as we snuck stolen moments in elevators and office hallways and wished for a bed, for privacy, for the tiniest bit of dignity. Which we probably didn't deserve.

22 Remember in the last essay, when I said my partner threatened to cheat on me? In truth, I cheated on him. Does that make all the details in that essay null and void? Do you still believe me?

I nodded, even as I thought about the word. Final. The final thing, the final step. The final act. The final end. I pictured a hole in the ground, a mixed ash heap.

I looked at the shape of you. A man like so many others, your bony tusks of shoulders and solid-wood chest.

You breathed, a heavy breath humid with want.

I traced your shape with my fingers. I felt your muscle and tissue, identified each of the quadrants. I pressed down to your bones underneath. I pressed hard and you gasped.

*Let me move you*, you said as you grabbed for my hips.

I wondered if I'd gotten lost somehow, if you were Graham, and I was back home, having our weekly sex, where I dreamed of anonymous cocks and slick cunts, made the sounds that he knew and expected, so we could have a moment that felt true. I wondered if I was dreaming, or dead, or broken.

So I climbed on top of you, pushed you inside me.

You felt like any other man, all the other men.[23] You felt like men I loved, and those I didn't. I shifted to let all of you in, to feel something new. To feel your soul, perhaps, matching with mine. You smiled, and I looked away, down, at where we joined. I watched our bodies move, up and down, in and out. What every animal did to live. I wondered if we were just animals in heat, rutting to stay sane and alive. I wondered if that was love. All the fuss, the fantasies, the foreplay, the flirting, all the things we told ourselves meant something; maybe it was all nothing.

With you inside me, I wanted to see inside you. Open you up and see all there was of you. Why did I want you? Why you? Was it you, or could it be anyone? I wanted to split you open, crack you along the spine, examine you. Find your soul that had to be my match. I wanted to tear back skin and bone, find what I loved and needed, and crawl inside next to it. Get stapled in and never leave.

As we got to the end, I wanted you to break me. Rip me to shreds so Graham wouldn't recognize me. Tear me in two from sacrum to skull, ensure no child could live inside me.

23 Even in my imagination, I posited reality tinged with disappointment.

But more than that, I wanted to break you.[24] Punch my hand straight through your skin, snap the rib cage, slap aside the lungs and heart and spleen, grip your thoracic as a rein, ride you to *finally*. I wanted to destroy you, so this moment, this breaking, this desperate act, would be erased.[25]

I breathed, and you breathed. I squeezed my legs around your hips. So that no matter where I really was, who you really were, I could try to meld my shape to yours. Transform into a body with a soul.[26]

—

In our apartment, the night of our last fight, Graham paced. From my spot on the floor, back against the brick wall, arms cinched around my legs, I counted off the complaints as they came. I was selfish, I was broken, I was a child, I was a drunk. No one in their right mind would want me. Would believe me.

—

After you fell asleep that night in the hotel, I closed my eyes and opened them, over and over. The shapes and shadows behind my lids were the same as those in the room. I thought I remembered a king bed with a cushioned headrest; a brittle, starchy wingback chair; a severe square desk; a hutch with TV eye. Paintings of daffodils and fox hunts.[27]

I wasn't sure if I was awake or asleep.

24 Even in my imagination, I saw destruction.

25 Nothing will make you feel more animal, more raw, more primal, than fucking someone you're not supposed to.

26 Poetic, yes? All because I've had a decade to think about it, to sort through. At the time all I knew was this: I loved him, I wanted him, and that was wrong. It was the first time I felt seen, the first time someone didn't define love as control. But it didn't matter: the right kind of love was with the man waiting at home, the man I was increasingly afraid of.

27 In fiction, you can merge things. Take settings and moments from other timelines, insert them where they didn't happen, all for a better story. This room, this strange sensation, came from another night, another man. Another country. A moment when I realized I had no idea who this person truly was. And the fright, the terror, that comes with that realization.

You were breathing next to me, slow and calm. I imagined your breath cut a path through the room, like a smoker's carbon monoxide trail. It swelled and stretched, your breath. I smelled sweat and sulfur behind it, tasted the acid tang of it.

You were breathing next to me. Then you weren't.

—

"Lucky," Graham said. Feet pacing. Eyes rolling. Hands clenching. He said I was lucky. Because what would I do otherwise? What would happen if we split up?[28]

—

You stood in the hall, next to the bathroom, and your breath rattled and hitched. Sinuses, I wondered. Or allergies. Things I didn't know about your body. You shushed yourself, and your breath marked the edges of sobs.[29]

My lids went up and down. I knew where I was, surrounded by austere furnishings and amateur paintings. But I also knew I was home, next to cold brick and cold disdain. And I knew I was somewhere between, not awake or asleep, not in the real world or this one.

I was just a body. So were you. If we had souls, they weren't here.

—

Graham waited, his breath fast, his mouth curling into a cry and a smile, back and forth.

"What would you do," he asked, "without me?"[30]

—

28 The constant fear of this refrain. The way you can explain inertia, and forgiveness, and faking happiness.

29 Because when it came down to it, he couldn't break up his family. I couldn't ask him to. There was no future, and no path forward without tears and pain.

30 The constant fear of this question too. But over time, the answer became more attractive, more hopeful. Something inside me knew the answer was simple. I would live.

In the hotel bed, I touched my breasts, my neck. My still-damp pubic hair, my hips.

You panicked in the hall.

I touched the pieces of me. The parts of flesh that added up to named shapes: shoulders, knees, elbows, chin. They were all here, unbroken and whole.

You probably thought about your family, the thing you complained about but needed, the thing that defined you, more than your job and your body and your dreams. You thought about temporary fixes, ejaculation as vacation. Expiration dates.

You already needed to be free of me. You already feared me, and what I might do.[31]

I was afraid of me too.[32]

—

"Maybe I should just leave," Graham said.

I stood up then. Graham saw something on my face, in the loosening of my shoulders. Relief, finally given new direction. Resolve.

He apologized. A first.

And I knew he understood me.

He said he took it back, said he wasn't serious. Said breaking up wasn't a serious thought. It wasn't what a serious couple did.

I moved around the apartment, nodding, quiet.

He followed me, pleading. Taking it back. Taking everything back.

"If I've broken this," he said, "what has my life been for?"[33]

—

31 Catch brief glimpses of this fear on a beloved's face, and the soul breaks. It dies.

32 It's a fearsome thing, to love so much you'll break the bounds of propriety. To become a cheater. A slut, a whore, a home-wrecker. You enter a new space, where you don't know yourself anymore, don't recognize who you are and what you will do. No wonder the adulterers among us are branded as the most dangerous of all.

33 A genuine question. He wanted to know. Needed to know. And because truth can mix with manipulation, he also wanted to hook me back, draw me further into his skin and his soul. Trap me.

You and I slept in our own hotel rooms.

We nodded to one another the next morning, and boarded our flight, and went home to our spouses.

I listened to Joy Division in my car, outside my apartment building. I could find my way back to Graham. I had to. Souls didn't have a match; if they did, mine was Graham. It had to be.[34]

—

But after that last fight, I knew there were no souls. It was only my body that had fit with another, and it was only my body that kept me in a relationship of pain.

So I left Graham.[35] That morning after our last fight. Snow covering the ground and freezing. Some of the stacks of snow still packed and unmelted months later.[36]

—

I left the spa, joined the competing hotel, where you didn't haunt the halls.[37]

—

After a few months at my new job, another therapist, a tiny woman with strong knuckles and wisps of black hair on her lip and chin, pointed at my shoulders. She said I needed to break those up.

I didn't know how long it had been since I had lain on a table. My body was rounder, my skin dull and flaky. The places where my joints connected

34 We force ourselves to love, coerce ourselves, to feel part of the world.

35 Did I leave my partner because I cheated? No, and yes. No, because everything I said about his behavior was true. Yes, because being loved by someone else in a way that celebrated me rather than controlled me gave me new sight.

36 In fiction, you can mold. Reality is condensed; separate events folded into one, fantasy blended into truth. I'm sometimes not fully sure where the fiction and nonfiction lie in this story.

37 We never told. We pretended it didn't happen. We pretended so well, so hard, that for many years I thought I may have imagined him. Imagined us. We pretended so well, so hard, I felt myself shift from a state of truth and reality to somewhere else: a hallucination, a mental deterioration. A story of my own making.

bones creaked and cracked. I turned the lights in the room down further before slipping naked under the sheet.

She went straight for my neck, kneading with those knuckles. She found a big nodule along the right side, and when she touched it, I pictured the gnarled knot of a tree trunk. Something without give.[38]

She used two knuckles, and wasn't gentle. The knot burst. I laughed, a giant horsey laugh. Then I cried, a meaty, snotty cry. My body made its sounds and took up the space. And if it existed, my soul rose up into the air and ran free.[39]

38 This happened.

39 This story is nonfiction.

# Part 4 Weird Woman

# Shape Worn

In the last diet book I ever bought, the author is pictured at her kitchen island and in her garden. She's following the template of every would-be diet and wellness guru: smiling and serene, posing with artfully arranged food, inviting you into her perfect life.

When I purchased the vegan keto book, I noticed the sharpness of the author's collarbone. Her skeletal sticks of arms. Her hair that hung limp and greasy. The smile that didn't reach her eyes. There was something disturbing there, a message trying to reach me.

But I ignored it. She was promising me the fix for my fat. And that was all that mattered.

Just weeks before, my doctor said it was time. "Can't eat the same way you used to," she said, pointing to the extra fat around my middle. "That's just the awful fact of aging."

This was not news to me. I'd been increasingly frenzied at the gym, and increasingly brutal at home, cutting my calorie count to subsistence levels, to try and fight the fat back. It wasn't working; now that I was forty-one, my doctor said, my body wasn't listening to me.

So I scoured the internet, just as I'd done before. What would work this time? What would finally tame my body? I found keto, just as it was starting to become the fad du jour. The idea of hacking my body's fat-burning mechanisms, tricking it into burning away weight by cutting carbs down to nothing, was intoxicating.

I found the book. I tried it. And after a few weeks, my body finally said no.

The worst thing to be is fat; that's what I learned early. Fat people were the targets of ridicule in every movie, show, news program, and school classroom around us. Everywhere.

And at home, it was worse. Fat people were the butt of jokes in every family conversation, and the specter of a fate worse than death.

My mother, looking in a mirror, crying as she pinched at her thin body, terrified at any new softness.

My mother, my father, pointing out fat women on the street, in stores, at work, disgust wrapped around pointer fingers, loud laughter falling from their mouths.

My aunt, gaining significant weight and becoming the worst-case scenario, looking mournfully at her plate every Christmas as she talked about her latest diet.

If she could just lose the weight. If my mom could just keep it off. If my family could just make sure they didn't look like those people. Maybe everyone would feel better. Feel loved. Feel worth it.

I stuck with the vegan keto plan for a few weeks. I ate tons of oils and nuts and avocados. I limited my vegetables, and I cut out nearly every grain and carb. There was a short, strict list of allowed foods, and a long book of every other forbidden food.

As I ate this way, my head grew cloudy, my stomach knotted, my bones ached. I returned to the book again and again. Was I was doing it right? Should I feel this way? Stick with it, the author said. You'll feel terrible. That's just your body finally submitting.

After a couple weeks, sick and weak, ravenous, the inevitable happened: I broke down, and ate everything in sight.

And with my stomach full and my brain clear, I looked at the diet book again. The author's skin stretched to the point of breaking over protruding ribs. Her face, tentative, searching, pleading. Pale, wan, a waif who could barely lift her lips to smile. *Do what I do*, it said, *so my sacrifice will be worth it*.

Was this the ideal? Was this what I sought for my future?

The worst thing to be is fat: that's what I internalized from my family and society.

So I spent forty years trying to control the uncontrollable. A young girl in elementary school, frantically doing sit-ups so my crush might like me. A teen girl wishing I could afford the SlimFast the other girls poured into their milk cartons; a girl watching after-school specials about bulimia with longing. A young adult starving myself as I ran and ran, at track meets, on treadmills, on city streets. An adult, with a partner who called my thin body fat, the worst in a litany of things he called my failures. A past-her-prime woman offering her skinny, beat-down body to those who would take it, hoping to make it feel.

I could be weird, often odd, and that was dangerous. But I could also be thin, and that could give me the keys to the kingdom.

All the diets. The diets with names: Fat Flush and Low Carb and Whole Grain. The diets without names: Wellness and Mindfulness and Boot Camp. All of them, designed to reinforce that the worst thing to be is fat. All of them, designed to take my money and dignity. Then, when it failed, ensure I felt like the failure.

I consulted that diet book again. Looked at the author. Willed it all to make sense.

And here's the thing. As afraid as I was of not fitting in, of looking weird and dangerous, of revealing something biological and pathological, over the years I'd found radical identities that fit with my curiosity and questioning mind. Even better, offered their own rules and structure. I could still mimic and mask, and feel more authentic, while calling myself a feminist. And an atheist. And a child-free woman. A bisexual weirdo. And a vegan for God's sake, in the Midwest's land of meat and potatoes.

But by forty, I still had massive blind spots. Many with radical identities do. I didn't understand the extent of my privilege as a white, thin woman. I looked at the world so critically, yet I didn't think to challenge ideas of body size. The morality, the goodness assigned to thinness; the supreme failure associated with fat.

I put down the book with the haunted, haunting author.

And that's when, in some sort of fugue state, looking for another way, I found a "Body Trust" questionnaire. The questions were things I'd never asked myself before:

- How did you lose trust with your body?
- What experiences impacted your ability to feel at home in your body?
- Have you ever blamed [the diets] or have you always blamed yourself?
- How has your body helped you survive in the world?
- What would be possible if you decided your body wasn't the problem?

A long list of questions like these, inviting me to think, to critique, to use that intelligence I prized and those critical skills I was so proud of. To understand how I'd been duped.

The worst thing is fat, especially a fat belly.

My aunt had large breasts her third husband bought her; the rest of us in the family, though, had swollen nubs, barely visible. And because we didn't have big boobs, we had to have flat stomachs.

In my thirties I met a woman with a big belly, one who seemed unashamed, who walked with her belly out. I was awed and shocked. Later, she and I had sex, and I marveled at the belly, its smoothness, its softness. Her black skin, her coarse hair, her smell. All of her, worth adoration. A body and belly she delighted in and invited me to delight in.

But still, I didn't learn. I was terrified of my own belly and body. So I ran and ran and ran, and didn't eat, and first my hips screamed with agony, and then my knees. I ignored the pain. Because we must do this. We must fight our bodies. What else is there?

The worst thing to be is fat. But meanwhile, my body, the vast and terrifying landscape of it, screamed for attention for decades. It yowled for help from the terrifying pain of irritable bowel syndrome. With the heavy, heavy weight of depression on my frame. With the accelerating spin and jolt of panic and anxiety. With the big blank swaths of forgotten memory. With the bruising and nausea from fluorescent lights, certain smells, open offices, background hums. With the pain of living with love that causes pain.

All of it, abnormal; no one else seemed to have bodies in constant pain. All of it, increasingly worse, increasingly frequent and unbearable, increasingly weighty, until everyday tasks became harder and harder, until I picked at my skin and scalp and fingers, pulling flesh off my body, digging to find the root of the matter.

I couldn't control the screaming of my body. Even with all the alcohol and smoking, all the fucking and running, all the self-excoriation and desperation, the shrieking grew louder. So I squeezed tighter, hoping if I made my body smaller, it would be silenced.

After I finished that questionnaire, after I started to feel the edges of something like understanding and relief, I kept going.

I found Yr Fat Friend (later identified as author and podcaster Aubrey Gordon), who described the realities of living in a fat body and the parameters of our culture's phobias. I found Health at Every Size, a paradigm for medical care that validates all bodies. I found Sonya Renee Taylor, who said the body is not an apology. I found Christy Harrison, a nutritionist, author, and podcaster exposing the limitations of medical and healthcare approaches to fat. I found an entire world of fat liberationists on Instagram, and body neutrality teachers across the podcast and internet space.

From these teachers, I learned that diets fail over 90 percent of the time. I learned that diet and wellness organizations make billions a year based on that fact. I learned that there is little evidence that fat is actually the killer that health care and public policy has portrayed it to be, and antifat bias may have the most disastrous impact on health. I learned that body size is as random and unique as a person's shoe size or height, and equally as uncontrollable.

And then, I remembered that my body was hungry because it was keeping me alive.

So I let myself eat. I let my sore and broken body rest.

I gained weight. But suddenly, that didn't seem like the worst thing. Because then I saw how much time and energy I'd wasted.

The worst thing. Especially for women, fat is the worst. Because we need to be small, to take up as little space as possible. We need to spend all our time and energy and creativity and love and intelligence toward making our bodies fuckable.

And if we don't, if we take up space, if we critique that messaging and advocate for ourselves, if we use our voice, we're feminazis and hags. If we let our bodies grow, we're ugly and unlovable.

We must be distracted by the quest to be small, so real power will elude us.

But if we don't? We become something different. Even dangerous.

The worst thing happened: I got fat. I grew a big, round belly. My thighs rubbed together, and my hips grew thick. I formed back fat and armpit fat.

I got fat, and my body felt steadier, more secure. Less plaintive yowls and howls of pain.

Soon after, I learned I was autistic. And my body was finally heard. So many of us older undiagnosed women, filling up a bingo card of bodily conditions and mental health issues; all ways our bodies begged and pleaded to be heard, to be discovered.

I let my body rest. I let it tell me what it needed. I let it be exempt from all the rules I thought were necessary for survival. I let it feel safety, for the first time.

I know that many, including my family, view my weight gain as a moral failing. Pitiable laziness. I'm the fat aunt now.

I know that culture views my fatness as sad. A middle-aged woman who has let herself go.

But now I don't think about calories and macros, and the hours I will need to torture my body at a gym. I eat anything, without restriction. Over time the foods that I felt uncontrollable around have lost their thrall. I eat with more peace now, less frantic and anxious, an animal with eyes rolling in need and want.

My body is bigger than it's ever been. I have moments of sadness about that, vestiges of my upbringing and living in this world. I have moments of deep fear and frenzy, of shame. I remember my years of hiding my difference, and that desire, that need, still exists. It still sometimes tells me to change myself. To cut and scrape away at my shape.

But most of the time, considering my bigger body, I just feel . . . neutral. My body keeps me here, alive, able to breathe and smile and pet animals and eat good food and laugh and fuck and fight.

And in the years since I gave up dieting, I've had time and energy for so much more. I wrote five books and published three. I created podcasts. I write and create with a fever now, art sprouting forth from me after years of numbness.

I'm lit with incandescent rage at the way the world lies to us, but also burning with fiery hope that we might all find our way to this new place.

The worst has happened. And I'm free.

# Punk on the Page

It's 2005, and I'm at the Metro in Chicago. The club is a legendary mainstay, and the warped walls and concrete floors hold decades of spilled booze and sweat from punks, thrashers, goths, and shoegazers. We're blocks from Wrigley Field, where fans also scream their lungs out in joy, but we're worlds away from the sunstroke of afternoons watching baseball in the bleachers and on rooftops. Here, it's always night.

It's a weeknight, but I'm drinking vodka, and smoking my fifth cigarette in the last hour, because it's 2005 and you can still smoke in clubs. I'm with a friend, also named Amy, also chain-smoking and drinking. We're celebrating because we've survived another day of late-twenties adulthood, and because we're doing what we do best: watch people play music. We go to street fests in our neighborhoods, and we go to Lollapaloozas in Grant Park, and we go to tiny dive bars in the industrial corridor, and we go to big arenas in the suburbs. We've learned our concertgoing styles: I hang out on the outskirts of the crowd to avoid claustrophobia and panic; she pushes her way to the front, returning to me muddy and with torn clothing, telling stories of what the band looks like up close.

But tonight we're together in the middle of the crowd. We're waiting to see Sleater-Kinney.

At some point I realize this is the only time I've seen a band who is composed entirely of women. It's a strange observation; I've seen dozens, maybe hundreds of acts, and this has never happened.

There's an opening band, but I'll forget who it is as soon as they leave the stage. And then, there's a roar of fans that sounds like an accelerating heartbeat. We spot the trio of Corin Tucker, Carrie Brownstein, and Janet Weiss. Then, the crunch of discordant guitars and military drum, along with the soul-rending wails of Corin and Carrie's vocals, are fed through the walls of speakers and drive into our chests and skulls.

For two hours Amy and I thrash our heads and dance and sweat and spill our vodka and spew our smoke into the cloud above us.

There's a moment during the show when I think about writing again. That's something I haven't done since I abandoned my first novel, realizing it wasn't the beautiful thing I'd imagined in my head. But the sounds Sleater-Kinney make, the discord and broken noise that shouldn't be melodic, and the way they look playing, powerful and terrible, there's something stirring in my head, a desire to capture a story that's as dark and beautiful as what they do. Along with an idea about how to do it.

But the impulse and the idea go away with the vodka and the noise. And in a few months, Sleater-Kinney will break up. But not tonight. Tonight, they're magic. Like I wish I could be.

It's 1992, and I'm a sophomore in high school. I go to school with 2,000 kids from the poor side of a dying town in a dead-end state. I go to school with the kids of plumbers and cashiers, cops and factory workers, and the Vietnamese and Laotian refugees from the 1970s. My high school years, my parents tell me, will be the best time of my life.

I hate this time in my life. I'm smart, and I'm quiet, and I'm consistently baffled by social dynamics. So at this age I'm starting my pattern of gravitating toward the edges, hopping from the group of Laotian girls who call me their token white girl, to the group of photo and art geeks who give me copied cassette tapes of *The White Album*, to my track and cross-country teammates who are all a little loopy in our masochism.

Punk and indie music are my soundtrack for the turmoil inside. A deep, thrumming knowledge exists in me, wanting to reject the rules that say I must marry young and work till I drop and that is life. When I find this era's punk, Nirvana and Pearl Jam and the bands labeled "grunge," the music welcomes me, as it welcomes other misfits. Punk gives me a place to exorcise my frustration through noise and dance, and an understanding that normal isn't all it's supposed to be.

I don't yet think about the fact that all of the music that speaks to me is from males. I don't think about the fact that it's loud, and snarling, and angry, and right—but it's not speaking from my voice.

But there are many girls and women who do. They're livid and longing for a home in punk. And a group of women's punk bands have pushed their way to the male-dominated stage with raging sounds and razor-sharp lyrics. Bikini Kill, Bratmobile, Heavens to Betsy, and later Sleater-Kinney; their music is loud, brash, and powerful. This punk has songs for and about girls, full of anger about sex, bodies, and the rules we're given.

This riot grrrl scene is more than music too. Girls and young women go to shows, write fanzines, come together in consciousness-raising groups, and get political and active. They call for a revolution, girl-style now.

I'm the ideal demographic, a teen during this movement for young women. But I'm not cool enough or connected enough to be aware of it. I'm a loner, raised to view other women as competition. I hide my frustration and confusion and budding anger, knowing there is no place for it, in my family, in the world; the only place is my bedroom, where my boom box pulses with male punks from Seattle and Georgia.

So I won't find riot grrrl until the moment is past, as a young college grad in a new city, working at a titan of capitalism by day, raging at shows or in my apartment by night. I will find riot grrrl when I'm no longer a girl, yet still seethe with the rage of what our world does to girls.

But around this time, I do have an experience I'll remember, pointing the way.

I must make a choice in my social studies class. Since it's an election year, and Iowa has a unique position in the national election circuit, I must choose a campaign to work on, or a local cause to get involved with, for a final project. Without a lot of thought, I choose the Equal Rights Amendment campaign, orchestrated by a coalition of political and social organizations.

While the national campaign had failed when I was a kid, this effort sought to add an amendment to Iowa's state constitution.

Simple tasks are what they give me in the sterile campaign headquarters near the airport. I go mute when I have to talk to people, so after a couple times of sweating through staffing the phones, I'm mostly stuffing envelopes and running errands. It's easy, and honestly kind of boring. Perhaps because I assume that this campaign will coast to victory. Why wouldn't the simple addition of "and women" to our constitution's promise of equality pass? It's logical, rational, and it seems almost silly that it hasn't been added already. The whole exercise feels like a school assignment, one reenacting a historical battle that's already been won.

So when the measure fails, voted out by people still scared that feminism will ruin the world and turn women lesbian and witchy, it seems like a shitty joke. It seems like I've time-traveled to the past of our history books, where women were property.

But then I start thinking about my mom, making fun of the woman at church who didn't take her husband's last name. Or my dad, who makes jokes about scaring off boys who might want to date me with his service weapon. I think about the times I mentioned I was working on this campaign, at family gatherings and school events, and was warned not to become a feminazi and burn my bras. I think about women's magazines at the grocery store, their monthly tips on keeping a flat stomach, hour-long processes to achieve a natural makeup look, and how to keep a man from straying. I think about what I'm taught to do when I'm alone: keep my keys between my fingers, hide bare skin, yell fire instead of rape because no one will come for the latter. I think about what I'm supposed to do: marry a man, have babies, ignore my hunger for food, connection, sex, and expression.

My anger and frustration grow. It gets harder to hide.

It's 2001. I'm twenty-four, and I've lived in a Chicago studio apartment near Boystown for a year. I'm working at a firm creating media strategy for cereal and allergy medication. I've made friends through proximity and alcohol, and I've made this city my home, and I've started dating the man I'll soon live with. Everything is fine.

But in other ways, I'm dying inside. This job is nothing that I pictured or wanted, and I feel dirty doing it. This city is vibrant and new, but in other ways it's like home: all the girls want to get married and have babies, if just a little later; all the people live in deeply divided color lines; my boyfriend says he understands me, but I know, even if I don't admit it to myself for ten long years, that he doesn't respect me.

Most nights I go home to my apartment and listen to music. I surf Napster and other music transfer sites, downloading all the current music that's shocking me and energizing me: the White Stripes, the Strokes, the Yeah Yeah Yeahs. But I'm also catching up on music that I missed in my pre-internet adolescence. On my massive computer monitor, I turn up the Stooges and the Ramones, the Slits and X, Sleater-Kinney and Bikini Kill, and jump around my apartment, dispelling the corporate air from my lungs and shaking out the animal grease that layers this city like sediment and forgetting about the tiny salary that won't pay my bills. I'm a girl again, the girl I wanted to be.

It's around this time my parents tell me they're getting a divorce, now that my brothers are graduating high school. Mom and Dad are not those high school kids anymore, the ones who got married and had babies, the way you're supposed to. I'm shocked for a moment, the sharp jab of a needle taking blood. But then I breathe. I've seen their fights, heard their complaints, know they barely tolerate each other. I know the secrets they think I don't.

All their rules, the ones stated and modeled. The ways I should live. They've broken them.

After their call, I listen to punk. After work gets more and more untenable, I listen to punk. After my boyfriend and I fight, I listen to punk. I'm surrounded by boxes and lines, and I listen to punk.

It's 2004. While I've always been obsessed with music, I've never desired to make it. Instead, I want to live loud by writing stories on the page. And now is the time I finally, officially, embark on a novel.

And almost immediately, it's shit. And I can't understand why.

I'm recognizing my anger more at age twenty-seven. The anger that comes from my family, as much as I try to deny it. But also the anger at the world that demands I breed, anger at people who demand I marry. Anger at a culture that tells me I'm odd, weird, wrong (and never tells me why).

There's much anger still to discover. Later I'll understand my anger at an increasingly tightening noose from my partner. I'll recognize my anger at being too queer and not enough, too young and too old, too loud and too quiet. I'm unnatural, repulsive, deviant. And angry about it.

But now, at my tiny desk in the apartment I share, I'm writing my first novel. Despite the anger and passion I'm feeling, the pages feel empty and hollow, a poor mimic of the books I love, a bland echo of the music that drives me. There is some sort of magic that I can't access.

I try everything. In the few free hours outside of work, I take one-off classes found in the classifieds of the *Chicago Reader*. I attend sketchy workshops in a mansplaining dude's apartment. I borrow books that promise to teach me what I'm not learning, books I close in defeat and pile out of sight. I outline, and re-outline, and write on notecards, and abandon the notecards, and fill out worksheets, and write backstories and character profiles, and write and rewrite, again and again and again.

And as I try to pay my bills and not get fired, I also try to break into a publishing world I don't understand, a world of generational wealth and snobbery and conflicting rules and gatekeepers. I research literary agents and write letters. I pore over magazines that offer smug advice from people who have been published. I learn I should go back to school, uproot my life, and live on . . . what? How do people do these things without even the shaky salary I have?

For years I do this. I struggle, and I strive, and I get rejected, and I hurt. All my intelligence, my nonstop reading, my bottled emotion and denied anger—none of it helps, none of it works.

Then, around the time things turn really bad with my partner, I finally give up. And I take my failure into myself. I'm a failure. I can't do the one thing I've always wanted to do.

My anger—it turns inward.

It's 2006, and 2008, and 2010, and 2012, and 2014. For years, I silence myself as a creative writer. I turn back to punk as my outlet. And I go to shows instead.

I go to Lollapaloozas, massive multiday festivals in Grant Park filled with known and unknown bands. I go to big venues, the Riviera, the Aragon, the Congress Theater, the Chicago Theatre. I go to small venues, the Vic and Schuba's and the Metro. I go to ballparks, Comiskey and Wrigley. I go to street fests and pop-up stages, to rooftops and basements.

I drink, and dance, and drink, and smoke, and drink. I feel the thump of reverb and bass and drum in my chest and heart and head. I tell myself that is enough.

For those years, I focus on my career as an advertising and communications writer and ignore the impulse to write creatively. I try to feel fulfilled and excited by that career, and instead feel disconnected and disillusioned. I burn out, and break down, and blow up my life.

I feel both empty and full of rage.

Then. I go to another show.

It's 2015, and I'm at the Slowdown in Omaha. The club is small, but the warped walls and concrete floors hold decades of spilled booze and sweat from the young punks and the aging ones. Like me.

I'm drinking vodka again, but I'm not smoking, because you can't do that anymore in clubs. Plus, nearing forty, I'm thinking about my health more and more. Amy is here with me, and she's drinking vodka, and she's also nearing forty, and she's a mom to a two-year-old.

The impossible has happened: Sleater-Kinney has reunited after nearly ten years.

We're in the club, and we've scouted spots together, near the back railing, and we're dancing along to an unknown named Lizzo, an opener who we fall in love with immediately.

In moments, I feel the small comfort I've started to feel more regularly. The comfort that comes from realizing no one cares about women in their forties. And the freedom in that. It's like I'm old enough to finally be the girl I wished I could be—utterly unruly and free.

Sleater-Kinney comes on. These women have come back together to create their art, and we, the women in this crowd, and the men, and the ones in between, we are hungry to receive it.

We dance, and scream, and sing, and drink, and smile, and cry, and laugh.

As I expel the dust of a decade, I realize I want to write again. I need to write again. And I've survived much, so much. I have stories to tell, and with the benefit of age, perhaps a way to tell them.

When Sleater-Kinney play "Dig Me Out" at the end of their encore, I feel as if the song tears from my chest, as if it's been there all this time, waiting for me to sing it at the top of my lungs, waiting for this moment when I see them and they hear me.

When Carrie and Corin and Janet leave the stage, we're drenched in sweat. My throat hurts. My feet hurt. But I feel like I leave with a little of their magic.

It's 2016, and 2017, and 2018. I write.

And I realize that my previous writing hid my anger and frustration behind a wall of artifice. I was writing splashy stories of singular women, the standard roles of ugly ducklings turned swans and misfits turned saviors. I was trying to be other writers, trying to tell stories that weren't mine to tell.

But after that concert, when I expelled my anger and felt free, I think about what happens with women and anger. If we don't exorcise our rage, it eats us alive. And if we do?

I try something new. I find part-time writing programs that don't require giving up your life; in a low-residency graduate program, I write, and read, and occasionally talk to a professor and fellow students online, all while I stay in my home and work.

The program requires two weeks in person each summer. And these sessions, they take me to Europe. I attend seminars and workshops in Dublin, Barcelona, and Vienna, writing and communing with the beautiful illusion of living abroad.

It's a terrifying investment in me, and a gamble, after so many strange classes and workshops and scams of the past. But it's time. And the experience, the travel, the stunning and terrible things I see, the amazing and awful people I meet, the pains and discomfort I feel—they knock me loose from that past failure.

I turn to short stories, the ideal place to work for controlled experiments. I write a story about a woman letting her anger out through extreme violence. Another about a woman whose anger turns magic. Another with anger transformed into revolution. Another who unlocks the key to happiness via rage.

And when I read my work this time, I feel the spirit of punk alive and well. Women who are deeply angry, genre-busting and deviant, and part of a vast collective and community of women telling their stories.

When I let myself go, and when I let my characters refuse to smile on demand, that's when I find my voice.

It's 2021, and I'm in my house. I'm watching a video of Sleater-Kinney performing their new album. It's just Carrie and Corin now, with a rotating cast of other players. Their music is slightly mellower, but still ferocious.

It's not a smoky club, and it's not a drowning-in-drink evening. It's just me, forty-four, living through a pandemic and panic attacks. I've finally learned who I am: an autistic woman who tried to hide, and who did it nearly flawlessly. One who is exceptionally, unabashedly angry.

When they begin to play, I dance, and scream, and sing, and cry, and smile.

I think of my first book. Named for Sleater-Kinney's album and song. A collection of stories about angry women, with songs of rage and terror and joy tearing from their chests. All of them, digging out from holes of their and society's making. Just like me.

When Sleater-Kinney leave the stage and I log off, nothing hurts and everything hurts. And I'm a little bit magic.

# Wyrd Sister

"If you are a woman and dare to look within yourself, you are a Witch."
—Women's International Terrorist Conspiracy from Hell (W.I.T.C.H.), 1968

Think back to when you were a kid. There was that old woman, remember? The one on your street or in your apartment building. The one who lived alone. The one you whispered about. The one your parents, your neighbors talked about. The weird one.

She was friendly enough, maybe, but she was different. Maybe a dead husband and grown kids. Maybe no kids or husband. Maybe some cats or dogs to replace them.

And "alone" plus "old" plus "woman" adds up in many child and adolescent minds as "witch."

What secrets were in that house? Weird ones, for sure. And sometimes you'd scare yourself, thinking about her, or walking past her house, which might have been in great shape or might have been run down. Or in bed, wondering if she was ever a kid, if she hated kids, if she never once thought about kids. And that in itself was odd. And then you thought about it, thought about all the adults you knew, and maybe you thought she might be an altogether different way to be a human.

Remember her?

That's me. I'm now the old lady living alone. The odd and strange one, the specter and the inspiration. I have tattoos, and often wear a scowl, and feed feral cats. I sometimes don't leave the house for days, even weeks. I'm queer, and whorish, and angry. I'm altogether witchy.

And maybe there's something infinitely fucking cool about that.

### "We Are W.I.T.C.H. We Are Women We Are Liberation We Are We"

The Women's International Terrorist Conspiracy from Hell was a feminist group based in New York City in the late 1960s. Their goals went beyond gender equality. Feminism wasn't just about women's rights, they said. Feminists should fight for many causes. They should work from an intersectional perspective, since queer rights, civil rights, disabled rights, all rights, benefited us all and chipped away at patriarchy.

Because ultimately all of us are in danger of burning at the stake.

W.I.T.C.H. embraced the weirdness of witchery. They were theatrical with their tactics. A public hexing of Wall Street and capitalism, dressed in pointy black hats and capes and carrying brooms. A mass protest at the New York Bridal Fair, wearing black veils and singing "here come the slaves, off to their graves."

But they were also fierce and pointed and earnest, one of few groups working to link the disparate entities in the radical underground. Like when they protested outside a New Haven women's prison, where pregnant members of the Black Panthers were denied prenatal care and forced to give birth under armed guard.

W.I.T.C.H. seemed to have preternatural predictive power, like the Weird/Wyrd Sisters, the Three Witches, who prophesied the destinies of the characters in *Macbeth*. With the things they targeted, and the messages they spread, W.I.T.C.H. anticipated the hard right turn in the 1980s, where feminism became co-opted into a mandate for women to work multiple jobs at work and home, to do it all, to smile and wear heels and revel in their equality, while dodging grabby hands and belittling bosses. They foresaw the early 2000s and their mercenary treatment of women celebrities, and the 2010s and their impossible standards of social media. They predicted the rise of hypocritical, trans-exclusionary feminism, where the most privileged scream without irony about groomers. They predicted the current harder right swing, with legislators passing increasingly incoherent laws against those who dare veer outside of the lines of gender, sexuality, and femininity. And in their quick dissolution under massive pressure, they predicted the rise and fall of riot grrrl, the condensed third and fourth waves of feminism, and movement after movement and movement.



> "W.I.T.C.H. is an all-women Everything. It's theater, revolution, magic, terror, joy, garlic flowers, spells. It's an awareness that witches and gypsies were the original guerillas and resistance fighters against oppression."

Historically, witches were women. Across time, across cultures, they were often considered wise women, experienced elders with knowledge of nature and its power to sustain and end life. They were healers, midwives, doulas; sometimes, they were spiritual advisers, connected to other worlds.

They were often alone: husbands gone, or never there; children aged and gone, or never given. They were independent, wholly responsible for themselves.

They were altogether weird, undeniably different from the others in the community. But they were also powerful.

Witches were the girls and women who didn't smile. The ones who couldn't hide their discomfort, their authenticity, their anger. Who chose not to hide. The ones who wouldn't arrange their features into something pleasing and comforting, wouldn't set aside their own needs and desires to make room for men's.

How dare they.

Witches were easy to burn. Their bodies cracked and peeled like any others'. But the idea of them, that was harder to destroy.

> "Your power comes from your own self as a woman, and it is activated by working in concert with your sisters."

Weird. The word is inherently witchy. It came to us from an Old English word, based on Norse mythology, where *wyrd* meant something akin to fate. Wyrd was the most powerful force in the universe; even gods had to submit to it. Wyrd was arbitrary, sometimes cruel. And those who determined wyrd were three women: the Norn. They carved the fates of all in the cosmos into the Yggdrasil tree, or in some stories, wove them with thread, cutting it when a person was to die. All their work was building toward the end of all things, which would come and leave nothing behind.

Did our fear of witches and all things weird come from this place? Did it assume that women held an unearthly power, an unfair power, an utterly abnormal power? Did it combine the Norse myth, and the Greek myth of Fates, and the Christian myth of Eve, and churn it all together into a "thou shalt not be woman and powerful, or thou shalt be a witch and thou shalt be burned for all to see"?

> "W.I.T.C.H. is the free part of each of us, beneath the shy smiles, the acquiescence to absurd male domination, the make-up or flesh-suffocating clothing our sick society demands."

I've long had a fierceness to me, an anger and principle and rawness that I've alternately embraced and hidden in shame. I've said no to much that is normal, and embraced different identities. And each time, perhaps to justify my dangerous step outside the norm, outside my mask, I wanted to understand the history behind each choice, each aspect of identity.

When I named myself a feminist in my younger years, I started a lifelong reading adventure. I read about women's history, and feminist theory, and gender exploration.

When I discovered in my thirties that I am a bisexual and queer person, I started a new reading path. I read about queer history, and queer persecution, and how queerness is the most authentic way of being a human.

When I learned in my forties that I am autistic, I read the meager handful of books about autism in women. And then I looked broader, at the history of autism. And broader still, to the history of disability, beyond the trite, infantilizing narratives we're taught in school about broken people learning to function in our capitalist society.

And with each, always, history is a horror. It's misogyny and ignorance and genocide. Always, it comes back to one thought, one rallying cry for those who are normal against those who are different, for those who dare to name themselves: burn the witch.

"Guards will be there.
When the babies are born.
Guards will be there.
To take them away.
The State will decide
Who's 'fit' and who's 'not fit'
To guard and be guardian
Of mother and child . . ."

In the 1930s, before the war, before the death camps, the Nazi Party created Aktion T4. This policy authorized the euthanasia of disabled and institutionalized people, including those with the disability that was later called autism. Because after all, the disabled were *Lebensunwertes Leben*—life unworthy of life. They were a genetic and a financial burden on society and the state, and a dilution of the pure *volk*.

At first it was children under the age of three. Parents were convinced to send their children to pediatric clinics for special care; the clinics were secretly killing wards. Later, it was kids up to seventeen. Then it was adults. Anyone with neurological, developmental, or physical disabilities were not part of the future.

Some doctors chose quick deaths for their institutionalized; some chose to starve and torture them. Ten thousand kids died in the first wave. Seventy thousand adults died in gassing centers built for this purpose, centers later used for Jewish, Roma, and queer people. Experts estimate that a quarter of a million disabled people were killed in this way in the war years.

"Therefore, W.I.T.C.H. curses the State
And declares *it* unfit . . .
Oppressors:
The curse of women is on you."

Here in the United States, disabled history is also horrific. Throughout much of the twentieth century, families were encouraged to institutionalize their children and relatives who were incalcitrant, different, queer, odd. And the resulting asylums were hovels: overcrowding. Forced confinement. Abusive staff. Barbaric and involuntary treatments of lobotomies, insulin shock, electro shock.

They were places to send your broken kids and adults, and then forget about them.

In the 1970s, new meds and new politics meant all these people were kicked out, back into society. Ostensibly with community support; often with utter neglect. They appeared on streets, and in shelters, and formed a new subclass of society, the ones your eyes would glance over. Like they were optical illusions, hallucinations. Not real.

> "Whatever is repressive, solely male-oriented, greedy, puritanical, authoritarian—those are your targets."

Disability means weakness. Brokenness. Stupidity. Life unworthy of life. That message survived into my childhood, and into my adolescence, and well into my adulthood.

Autism is one of those disabilities that shows this plainly. Conspiracy believers, insisting that vaccines cause autism, are emboldened to speak loudly and cruelly because they believe autism to be a pitiable, terrible thing. Warrior parents, slapping bumper stickers on their cars and reveling in their martyrdom, are empowered because they say autism is an affliction, a curse, a sickness that won't let their real, normal child free. Employers are endowed with purpose and self-righteousness during autism awareness month, trotting out their autistic employees, showing they can actually do things, they aren't totally useless, they can produce just like the rest of us.

Because we all believe otherwise. Believing that autism is a problem needing to be solved. It's bad and must be stopped. It's ruin. It's so just *weird*. And it must be burned away.

> "Double, bubble, war and rubble,
> When you mess with women, you'll be in trouble.
> We're convicted of murder if abortion is planned.
> Convicted of conspiracy if we fight for our rights.
> And burned at the stake when we stand up to fight."

I'm forty-six, and in the early stages of menopause. I'm a woman who is no longer culturally relevant, since I'm not young, and not nubile, and not all the things that might make me fuckable and therefore slightly interesting. I'm a woman from Generation X, which has always been a blip between the more important Baby Boomers and Millennials. I'm a middle-aged autistic woman, who some refuse to believe exist. I'm the woman who is now expected to fade away, into the background, into the spaces between things. I'm the old woman down the street, living in a haunted house.

I've made myself invisible too. I erased myself daily, hourly, by the second, wearing a mask so I might appear like the rest of the world. Allowing myself some oddities, but working hard to compensate. And now that I know why, I find myself wanting only to feel safe and validated. To do the things I want to do. Which is selfish and weird.

But. What's wrong with being selfish and weird?

"You are a Witch by saying aloud, 'I am a Witch' three times,
and *thinking about that*."

Growing up, reading material at my home was limited. A few paperback Danielle Steel books for when Mom needed to believe in true love. The daily newspaper for when Dad needed to check the weather, the police activity, and the progress of the liberal-pinko-commie media takeover. And the stray magazine, like *Good Housekeeping*.

I read it all. Everything in the house, everything in the school library and the city library. Things meant for me, and much more that wasn't.

I absorbed it, the reading itself and the messages implicit within. So much so that when I was around ten, I wrote a parody of women's magazines called *Weird Woman*. I used spiral-bound notebook paper, the edges ragged and loose, and I included articles, quizzes, ads, and illustrations. The discerning reader could read about the epidemic of weirdness in an article, assess their weirdness with a quiz, then find the snake-oil solution with the facing ad. The admiring reader could send in a square reply card stating, yes, they would like to learn more, to receive a subscription to *Weird Woman*.

I thought my little zine was hilarious, and smart, and endearing. The truth of that is lost to time and trash.

But I do know that I handed it to my parents with searching eyes, everything in me screaming in silence. This is me, it said. This is what I can do. This is who I am.

Maybe I titled the thing wrong. Maybe I should have called it *Wyrd Women.*

"You make your own rules. You are free and beautiful."

I'm learning that "selfish" merely means "inconvenient" and "upsetting" to most people.

Selfish is not doing what you're supposed to do. And when you're a woman, you're supposed to marry, have children, and stay skinny and small. If you refuse, you're selfish.

Selfish is saying no. When you're a woman, you're supposed to prioritize everyone else over yourself. Your kids, your spouse, your country, your job. You are supposed to take on every request, every demand, every need, and break slowly and swiftly inside, and cover that up, and continue breaking while pretending that you're fully solid and strong. If you refuse, you're selfish.

Selfish is looking out for yourself. When you're a woman, you wait to build a life until you have all the components. If you build a life and a home for yourself and no one else, you're selfish.

Selfish is spending time on things you enjoy. When you're a woman, you are supposed to enjoy the things your partner, your kids, your friends, your parents enjoy, value those interests and enjoyments above your own. Even forget what you like and value. If you refuse, you're selfish.

Selfish is being someone unique and individual. Selfish is doing anything that reminds others they are not unique or individual. Selfish is living without a smile at the ready.

Selfish is not being normal. Selfish is choosing weird.

So maybe selfish is actually the best way to be.

"You can be invisible or evident in how you choose to make our witch-self known."

I used to be ashamed of anger. Watching the women in my maternal line, with their unpredictable anger and tears and combination of the two, I taught myself that emotion was weakness. That anger was a burden.

Age changed that, of course. Living in the world as a femme-presenting woman changed that. And learning that I struggled for forty-three years without the full picture of who I was changed that.

Why should anger be a shame? If you're not angry, are you alive?

I am weird, and I am selfish, and I live in the world. So I'm mad.

I'm mad that I worked for so many years to be less wild, less red. To shut down my anger and tears and raw rage in order to be more palatable to the world. To distance myself from the women I learned from.

I'm mad because the world says a sexual woman is a slut, and an exuberant woman a lush, and a woman who loves and hopes a basket case, and a woman who lives in the world pitiable.

I'm mad that women paired with anger is still so shocking. That it's still an ugly thing.

I'm desperately, painfully mad that medical bias said autism was only one thing, and for only one type of person, for most of my life. That I never had the context for how to live fully, without unnecessary pain.

And I'm livid that my mother and aunt and grandmother, and generations of women back and back, taught each other to be high-functioning. I'm mad that their only recourse, the only way to relieve pressure and tension, was to turn on each other, to turn on me, and to tear ourselves apart. I'm mad that because we never knew about autism, we never were able to understand each other, to connect, to do anything but internalize shame. I'm mad because we've never been able to communicate. I'm mad that I can't discuss all of this because decades of hurt and miscommunication and shame created a vast rift no one wants to cross.

I'm furious. And I'm less and less inclined to hide it. I'm less afraid of being unpalatable. Ugly. Weird. Other.

So now, I've become something new.

Or maybe something very old.

"You are a Witch by being female, untamed, angry, joyous, and immortal."

So here it is: I'm a Weird Woman.

I'm a Masked Woman. I'm a Trashy Woman. I'm a Bad Woman.

I'm big and loud. I'm depressed and occasionally suicidal. I'm a storyteller.

I'm a Wyrd Woman.

I like living alone.

I like the silence of a child-free house.

I like the loudness when I play punk music at the volume it deserves.

I like staying inside on hot summer days, and I like going outside on cold winter afternoons.

I like learning. I like reading. I like LEGO sets. I like playing piano. I like science fiction shows, and terrible '80s movies, and weird musicals like *Spring Awakening*. I like writing. I like telling stories.

I like going days, weeks, without talking to anyone. I like workdays with no conference calls. I like solitude. And, I also like day-drinking on my porch with my friends. I like happy hours at hotel bars.

I like listening to a David Bowie song, and clutching my chest at the exquisite beauty and sadness, feeling both pure joy and deep bittersweet pain.

I like catching one of my cats giving me a long slow blink, and feeling the upswell of love and companionship without words.

I like the aftermath of a therapy session full of tears, when I feel scooped out and filled in all at once.

I like that I built the strength to cut off contact with my mother. That I'm setting boundaries with my father and brothers.

I like knowing I'm just an animal, content in its grotesquery, who shits and fucks and has a body full of pus and bile and unfathomable mystery.

I like that I now know why some things have been so hard, and some things so easy, even if that means I'm considered broken.

I like that I'm weird, and I'm selfish, and I'm a bad daughter, and a bad sister, and often a bad friend and girlfriend.

Said a different way: I'm removing shame from my life. I'm easing off my mask. I'm accepting the black clouds and the desire for oblivion, as well as the riotous joy of life. I'm doing the things I truly like to do, spending time with the people who truly value me, and creating the life that works best for me. I'm honoring those who came before me who couldn't do this simple act of life.

"Double, bubble, war and rubble
When you mess with women, you'll be in trouble.
We curse your empire to make it fall—
When you take on one of us, you take on us all!"

I had a family I was born to, and they did their best. They taught me about normal, a definition based on their youth, their isolation, their midwestern upbringing, their working-class life. From them, and from the world they lived in, I learned what was normal for a female body, and what was normal for my mind. I learned normal as a seeker and loser of friends and romantic relationships. I learned normal, and I learned I was abnormal. So I learned to hide, to limit, to run and run and run.

And I have a family I chose. When I first joined, they called me lesbian-ish and witchy, which I didn't fully understand but knew felt right. They spotted me before I did. Maybe because they themselves are all shades of weird. Gay, lesbian, straight; child-free and blended families; book nerds and Broadway nerds. All of us in some way middle-aged queerdos. Normal has no place in this family. It has no value. So neither does hiding.

Normal means pain. It means genocide and gendercide. It means life unworthy of life. Who really wants, let alone survives, the norm?

"We are everywhere.

We are your sisters, your neighbors, your teachers, your bartenders, your mechanics, your check-out clerks, your drivers and your nurses.

We have always been here. We will always be here."

—W.I.T.C.H. PDX, 2016

W.I.T.C.H. didn't die. Even though the main collective phased out action and messaging by 1970, leaders went on to form other radical groups. Like the Jane Collective, helping women access safe abortions before it was legal.

Then, in 2016, after Donald Trump was elected president, W.I.T.C.H. resurrected. Covens opened in Portland, Boston, Chicago, and other cities.

Because the cry remains, and grows louder: Burn the witch.

But so does our reply: Just try it.

I've been burned, but I survived.

I exist, and I've always existed.

I'm queer, and we've always existed.

I'm autistic, and we've always existed.

I'm different. I'm weird. I'm inconvenient. We've always existed.

My inner witch is ready. My inner witch—angry, ugly, shrill, punk, feminist, anarchist, silly, so very weird—it's her time.

I'm casting spells by putting these words together. I'm working magic by creating a life worth living, beyond trauma, beyond normal, beyond all.

I'm the witch down the street. All will feel the joy and terror of witnessing me.

And you?

Your inner witch. Is she ready? Is it her time?

Join me, my wyrd sister. Let's howl at the moon. Cast spells and hexes. Strip naked and revel in our beautiful, disgusting bodies. Leave behind all that is normal. Defy all that we are supposed to be. Live in our haunted houses. Be big, and just, and fireproof. Become.

# Acknowledgments

Thank you to the editors of the following publications in which these essays, often in different forms, first appeared: "The Masked Woman" originally appeared in the *Miracle Monocle* 20 (Spring 2023): https://louisville.edu/miraclemonocle/issue-20/amy-lee-lillard; "Dead Souls" originally appeared as a fictional story in *Exile in Guyville* (Rochester, NY: BOA Editions, 2024); "Shape Worn" originally appeared as an essay, "The Best $15.79 I Ever Spent: My Last Terrible Diet Book," *Vox*, November 14, 2021: https://www.vox.com/the-goods/22776258/diet-culture-best-money-vegan-keto-book; "Punk on the Page" originally appeared as an essay, "Finding My Voice through the Rage of Punk Music," *LitHub*, October 22, 2021: https://lithub.com/finding-my-voice-through-the-rage-of-punk-music/.

Thank you to James McCoy, Susan Hill Newton, Allison T. Means, Maya M. Torrez, Laura Poole, Elizabeth Sheridan, Karen Copp, and all who work at and with University of Iowa Press. Thank you to Erin Kirk for her beautiful cover and page design.

Thank you to Kaitlin Ugolik Phillips and Melissa Faliveno. Thank you to Leann Waterhouse. Thanks to Jessica Kramer, who wrote about her experiences with late-diagnosed autism in *Bust Magazine*. Her article is the reason I found my name and why this book exists.

Thank you to the women and nonbinary and trans individuals in this late-diagnosed community, who create podcasts, books, content, and stories, all to help more of us find the answers to our lifelong questions. I hope this book will do the same.

Thank you to the suicide survivors, and the complex PTSD survivors, and all those who are fighting to be here. I see you.

Thank you to the women and the queer community who persist and resist, in the face of increasing acts of annihilation.

And thank you to my chosen family of friends.